AQA Religious Studies:

A2

Philosophy of Religion

Exclusively endorsed by AQA

Anne Jordan
Neil Lockyer
Edwin Tate

Nelson Thornes

Published in 2009 by:
Nelson Thornes Ltd
Delta Place
27 Bath Road
CHELTENHAM
GL53 7TH
United Kingdom

09 10 11 12 13 / 10 9 8 7 6 5 4 3 2 1

A catalogue record for this book is available from the British Library

ISBN 978 1 4085 1384 2

Cover photograph: Photolibrary/BrandX Pictures
Page make-up by Hart McLeod

Printed and bound in Spain by GraphyCems

The authors and publisher are grateful to the following for permission to reproduce
photographs and other copyright material in this book:
pviii Interfoto/Personalities/Alamy; p8 Fotolia; p10 iStockphoto; p13 Corbis; p21
Sistine Chapel Ceiling: *Creation of Adam*, 1510 (fresco) (post restoration) (detail) by
Michelangelo Buonarroti (1475–1564) Vatican Museums and Galleries, Vatican City,
Italy/The Bridgeman Art Library; p24 (top) *The First Landing of Christopher Columbus
(1450–1506) in America*, 1862 (oil on canvas) by Dioscoro Teofilo de la Puebla Tolin
(1832–1901), Ayuntamiento de Coruna, Spain/The Bridgeman Art Library; p25 David
Turnley/Corbis; p27 Dorling Kindersley; p33 *The Light of the World*, c.1851–3 (oil
on canvas) by William Holman Hunt (1827–1910), Keble College, Oxford, UK/The
Bridgeman Art Library; p35 Neil Tingle/Action Plus; p49 *Mona Lisa*, c.1503–6 (oil
on panel) by Leonardo da Vinci (1452–1519), Louvre, Paris, France/Giraudon/The
Bridgeman Art Library; p57 Greyson scale used by kind permission of Professor
Bruce Greyson; p57 *The Ascent into the Empyrean or Highest Heaven*, panel from an
altarpiece thought to be of the Last Judgement (oil on panel) by Hieronymus Bosch
(c.1450–1516), Palazzo Ducale, Venice, Italy/The Bridgeman Art Library; p63 Mark
Pearson/Alamy; p80 Roger Viollet Collection/Getty Images; p87 Fotolia.

Every effort has been made to contact the copyright holders and we apologise if any
have been overlooked. Should copyright have been unwittingly infringed in this book,
the owners should contact the publishers, who will make corrections at reprint.

Contents

AQA introduction   iv

Introduction to philosophical reasoning   vi

Unit 3B	Philosophy of Religion	1
Chapter 1	The ontological argument and the relationship between reason and faith	1
Chapter 2	Religious language	21
Chapter 3	Body, soul and personal identity	39
Chapter 4	The problem of evil	63
	Summary of key points	97
	Examination-style questions	107
	Index	108

AQA introduction

Nelson Thornes and AQA

Nelson Thornes has worked in collaboration with AQA to ensure that this book offers you the best support for your AS or A Level course and helps you to prepare for your exams. The partnership means that you can be confident that the range of learning, teaching and assessment practice materials has been checked by the senior examining team at AQA before formal approval, and is closely matched to the requirements of your specification.

Blended learning

Printed and electronic resources are blended: this means that links between topics and activities between the book and the electronic resources help you to work in the way that best suits you, and enable extra support to be provided online. For example, you can test yourself online and feedback from the test will direct you back to the relevant parts of the book.

Electronic resources are available in a simple-to-use online platform called Nelson Thornes *learning space*. If your school or college has a licence to use the service, you will be given a password through which you can access the materials through any internet connection.

Icons in this book indicate where there is material online related to that topic. The following icons are used:

Learning activity

These resources include a variety of interactive and non-interactive activities to support your learning.

Progress tracking

These resources include a variety of tests that you can use to check your knowledge on particular topics (Test yourself) and a range of resources that enable you to analyse and understand examination questions (On your marks ...).

Research support

These resources include WebQuests, in which you are assigned a task and provided with a range of web links to use as source material for research.

Study skills

These resources support you in developing a skill that is key for your course, for example planning essays.

When you see an icon, go to Nelson Thornes *learning space* at www.nelsonthornes.com/aqagce, enter your access details and select your course. The materials are arranged in the same order as the topics in the book, so you can easily find the resources you need.

How to use this book

This book covers the specification for your course and is arranged in a sequence approved by AQA.

AQA Unit 3B, Philosophy of Religion, is covered in the first four chapters of the book. This encompasses: The ontological argument and the relationship between reason and faith; Religious language; Body, soul and personal identity; and The problem of evil.

A further chapter introducing Unit 4, Religion and human experience, is available to download as a free PDF from the Nelson Thornes website at www.nelsonthornes.com/religion_unit4.pdf. Additional online resources covering the whole of Unit 4, Religion and human experience, are delivered on our exciting new online environment, Nelson Thornes *learning space*. Visit www.nelsonthornes.com/learningspace for more information.

Learning objectives

At the beginning of each section you will find a list of learning objectives that contain targets linked to the requirements of the specification.

The features in this book include:

Key terms

Terms that you will need to be able to define and understand.

Links

These refer you back to other points in the book which consider similar points

Think about

Short points for discussion within small groups or your class.

Activity

Things for you to do that will reinforce the information you have just learned.

Take it further

Tasks for you to complete if you want to stretch your knowledge or understanding of an issue.

AQA Examiner's tip

Hints from AQA examiners to help you with your study and to prepare for your exam.

AQA Examination-style questions

Questions in the style that you can expect in your exam. AQA examination questions are reproduced by permission of the Assessment and Qualifications Alliance.

Learning outcomes

At the end of each chapter you will find a list of learning outcomes. These remind you what you should know having completed the chapter.

Summary of key points

The unit finishes with a summary of key points from the previous four chapters.

Web links in the book

Because Nelson Thornes is not responsible for third party content online, there may be some changes to this material that are beyond our control. In order for us to ensure that the links referred to in the book are as up-to-date as possible, each web site is accessible through this Nelson Thornes site: www.nelsonthornes.com/aqagce.

Please let us know at **webadmin@nelsonthornes.com** if you find a link that doesn't work and we will do our best to redirect the link, or to find an alternative site.

Introduction to philosophical reasoning

What is the nature of philosophical argument?

This is a difficult question to answer but a starting point might be that the word 'philosophy' comes from the Greek word meaning 'love of wisdom'. The nature of philosophy in the simplest terms is a way of thinking in which philosophers seek wisdom through the acquisition of knowledge, experience and understanding. Philosophy asks questions about the structure of the world and the meaning of human life using logical investigation and critical inquiry to present arguments supported by **reason**.

Philosophers are seeking proof that what they believe is true and use argument to support their beliefs. Their argument will begin with a **proposition** and seek to reach a conclusion that is proved true by the propositions. Proof may be defined as:

> an argument which starts from one or more premises, which are propositions taken for granted for the purpose of the argument and argues to a conclusion.

Richard Swinburne, The Existence of God, *1993*

A proof may be represented by a **premise** or premises that reach a conclusion. For example, there is life on Mars; God exists; or 'bi' means 'two' so a bicycle has two wheels.

Logical arguments

Logical argument might be described as a method of reasoning aimed at proving an argument true or false. Logical arguments may be divided into two types:

- deductive arguments
- inductive arguments.

Deductive arguments

Harriet Harris states that 'proof can be acquired only from valid deductive reasoning', in her article 'Proof and Probability in Arguing for God's Existence'. Deductive arguments are also known as **a priori** arguments. Deductive arguments do not depend on experience but on analysis to reach a logical conclusion. It is the use of logic and knowledge that prove statements true or false. Such a proof in deductive arguments is a statement that cannot be false; for example, four plus four equals eight. This is known to be true as it is accepted in mathematics that this is the correct answer. Therefore, the proof is said to be **logically necessary** because it would be absurd to suggest an alternative conclusion based on the premises. Similarly we would know that four plus four equals ten is untrue because in mathematics it is accepted that four plus four equals eight.

Key terms

Reason: the use of logic to come to a conclusion.

Proposition: a statement, assertion or theory that is seeking to prove the argument under discussion.

Premise: a statement presumed true within the context of the argument for the purposes of arguing to a conclusion.

A priori: an argument that uses logic to prove an initial definition to be correct. The statement is examined to prove it true or false.

Logically necessary: a statement that consists of a set of premises and a conclusion that cannot be disputed.

Deductive arguments also apply to the accepted meaning of words. To state that a quadruped is a four-legged animal is true because that is the accepted definition of the word, as is the statement that a triangle has three sides. These statements are called **tautologies**.

A priori arguments are deductive arguments because it is possible to deduce from the statement itself whether it is true or false without having to use experience as in an **a posteriori** argument.

Inductive arguments

Inductive arguments are also known as a posteriori arguments. Inductive arguments are based on experience and therefore are the opposite of a priori arguments where things are knowable independently of experience. The premises of inductive arguments have to be tested using evidence based on experience or experiment to prove the truth of the conclusion.

> Arguments which draw on or must be tested by evidence are inductive arguments, and they do not yield proof. They yield **probability**.

Harriet Harris, Proof and Probability in Arguing for God's Existence, *2004*

Arguments as 'valid' and 'good'

> A valid or sound deductive argument is one in which the conclusion necessarily follows from the premises.

Harriet Harris, Proof and Probability in Arguing for God's Existence, *2004*

If the conclusion of a deductive argument does not follow from the premises then it is not a valid argument. Sometimes deductive argument can be valid but may not be considered a 'good' argument because it is possible to challenge concepts contained within the premises.

Inductive arguments are based on probabilities and therefore a valid inductive argument is one in which the conclusion is probable based on the premises. Inductive arguments may be valid, but as with deductive arguments they may not be a good argument. Inductive arguments would not be considered good if the truth of the premise(s) is not known to those who do not accept the conclusion.

Reductio ad absurdum arguments

Reductio ad absurdum arguments are logical arguments that seek to prove things true by contradiction. The argument is presented in such a way that an absurd or ridiculous conclusion is reached to prove that the original claim must have been wrong as it has led to this absurd result.

■ Analytic and synthetic propositions

In his work *The Critique of Pure Reason*, Kant divided propositions into two types:

■ analytic propositions
■ synthetic propositions.

■ **Key terms**

Tautologies: statements that are necessarily true, either because they are logical or mathematical in nature, or because they are truisms and true by definition. For example, a circle is round. A posteriori: an argument that is based on experience rather than logic; the opposite to an a priori argument.

Probability: chance, or likelihood, that a certain conclusion is true.

Reductio ad absurdum: Latin for reduction to absurdity. In philosophy the aim is to disprove an argument by showing that the consequences of the proposition are absurd, or that the conclusion reached is the opposite of what we were aiming to prove.

■ **Think about**

Look at the following deductive argument:

■ Abortion is murder.
■ Murder is wrong.
■ Therefore abortion is wrong.

This is a valid argument as the conclusion follows from the premises. However, some people may not consider it a 'good' argument. Why do you think that this is the case?

■ **Think about**

Look at the following inductive argument:

■ The universe was caused to exist.
■ Things exist because they are caused.
■ The universe was caused.

This is a valid argument as the conclusion is probable based on the premises. However, some people may not consider it a 'good' argument. Why do you think that this is the case?

Kant divided propositions into the analytic and the synthetic

Analytic propositions

Analytic propositions are associated with deductive arguments. These are propositions in which the predicate (the part of the proposition that tells you what something is, does or has) is contained within the subject content. Examples of analytic propositions are:

- All spinsters are unmarried.
- A triangle has three sides.
- A ring is a circle.

Synthetic propositions

Synthetic propositions are associated with inductive arguments. Synthetic propositions are propositions in which the predicate is not contained within the subject and so it is necessary to use evidence to prove the proposition true or false. Examples of synthetic propositions are:

- Jane is a spinster.
- John plays the triangle in a percussion band.
- Susan's engagement ring is a circle of gold.

Analytic propositions: these are necessarily true independent of fact or experience.

Synthetic propositions: these are propositions in which the predicate is not part of the meaning or definition of the thing. To prove the proposition true or false some form of experience or experiment is necessary.

Philosophy of Religion

1 The ontological argument and the relationship between reason and faith

Learning objectives:

- to understand the ontological argument as presented by Anselm and Descartes

- to understand the key objections to the ontological argument

- to evaluate the success of the argument as proof of God's existence

- to evaluate how far the argument makes it reasonable to believe in God

- to assess the relationship between faith and reason as reflected in the ontological argument

- to assess the significance of the success or failure of the argument for faith.

Key terms

The ontological argument: the arguments for the existence of God based on the idea that the very fact that we have a concept of God must mean that He exists.

The God of classical theism: this holds that God is an absolute, eternal, all-knowing (omniscient), all-powerful (omnipotent) and perfect being. God is related to the world as its cause, but is unaffected by the world (immutable). God is transcendent, meaning that God exists outside the constraints of space and time.

ℹ️ The ontological argument for the existence of God

Proof of the existence of God would demonstrate that the statement 'God exists' is true. **The ontological argument** has the form of a deductive proof. It is an example of an a priori argument. This is because it seeks to prove the existence of God from the understanding of the attributes of **the God of classical theism**.

Activities

1. Write a definition of what you understand to be the nature of God.

2. Compare your definition with the definition given by other people in the group.

Ontological argument as a term refers to a number of arguments within one school of thought. The two principal contributors to the classical ontological argument are:

- St Anselm of Canterbury (1033–1109)
- René Descartes (1596–1650).

💡 Anselm's version of the ontological argument

Some philosophers do not consider that Anselm's *Proslogion* was presented as an argument for the existence of God. They believe that it was more likely that it was a prayer to God in which Anselm was offering a devout exploration of his faith and seeking greater understanding of God. Therefore, it may be that later philosophers used Anselm's points as an argument for the existence of God in his work the *Proslogion*, which translates as *Discourse on the Existence of God*.

Anselm's intention in the *Proslogion* was to offer arguments that would establish not only the existence of God but also the various attributes that Christians believe God possesses. Anselm's version of the ontological argument is in two parts (although Anselm never uses the term 'ontological argument'). There is a debate among scholars as to whether Anselm himself saw two forms of the argument or whether this is how 20th-century philosophers who have developed the ontological argument saw it.

The first part of Anselm's argument

In the *Proslogion*, Anselm defined God as '*aliquid quo nihil maius possibit*', that is 'that than which nothing greater can be thought'. It is from this definition that the first part of his argument is developed. Anselm meant that God is the greatest being that can be thought of; that is, a being that cannot be improved upon. To think of a greater being means that being is God.

■ Key terms

Atheist: someone who denies the existence of God or gods.

■ Key philosopher

St Anselm of Canterbury (1033–1109)
He was a medieval Italian theologian and philosopher who was once Archbishop of Canterbury. He proposed a famous version of the ontological argument.

■ Link

Look back to pvii of the Introduction and remind yourself of the differences between a priori and a posteriori arguments, and what is meant by inductive and deductive proof.

■ Take it further

Use the library and/or the internet to find out more about Anselm and Descartes.

Read Anselm's complete argument in *Proslogion 2*.

Anselm refers to the reference in the Book of Psalms that states, 'The fool has said in his heart, "There is no God"' (Psalm 14:1; 53:1). Anselm sees the absurdity of the fool's position as there is a contradiction in that the **atheist** (the fool) understands the definition of God as the greatest conceivable being but at the same time rejects this concept of God by denying the existence of such a being.

> And, indeed, we believe that thou art a being than which nothing greater can be conceived. Or is there no such nature; since the fool hath said in his heart, there is no God? [Psalm xiv. 1]. But, at any rate, this very fool, when he hears of this being of which I speak—a being than which nothing greater can be conceived—understands what he hears, and what he understands is in his understanding; although he does not understand it to exist.
>
> *Anselm*, Proslogion 2, *1077–8*

The fool therefore:

■ understands the claim that God exists
■ does not believe that God exists.

Anselm seeks to show that the fool is wrong in saying that God does not exist as anyone who understands what it means to say that God exists must have knowledge of God. Anselm argues that whatever is understood *must* exist in the understanding, so that than which nothing greater can be conceived exists in the understanding; even the atheist has this understanding even if only to dismiss the existence of God.

'In one's understanding' and 'to understand'

Anselm makes a distinction between an object 'in one's understanding' and 'to understand' that the object exists. What Anselm means is that there is a difference between saying that something exists in one's understanding and saying that one understands (or believes) it exists. For example, unicorns exist in people's understanding; but people understand that unicorns do not exist. However, before an artist paints a picture he understands in his mind what he is going to paint. The painting therefore exists in the artist's understanding, and then when he has painted it the picture is in both his understanding and reality.

> For it is one thing for an object to be in the understanding, another to understand that the object exists. For when a painter first imagines beforehand what he is going to make, he has in his understanding what he has not yet made but he does not yet understand that it is. But when he has already painted it, he both has in his understanding what he has already painted and understands that it is.
>
> *Anselm*, Proslogion 2, *1077–8*

In arguing that God is 'something than which nothing greater can be conceived', Anselm is stating that if God exists in the mind (*in intellectu*) alone then a greater being could exist in both the mind and the reality (*in re*). This being would then be something than which nothing greater can be conceived and would therefore be God. The conclusion is therefore that God must exist.

> There exists, therefore beyond doubt something than which a greater cannot be imagined both in the understanding and in reality.
>
> *Anselm*, Proslogion 2, *1077–8*

The use of reductio ad absurdum

If Anselm is presenting an argument for the existence of God then Anselm is using reason to prove God exists. He has used the method of reasoning, *reductio ad absurdum*, to prove that God exists. This is how the argument works:

- Suppose God only exists in one's understanding.
- Then God could be greater by existing in reality.
- This means a greater God is possible – one that exists in reality.

This last statement would be a contradiction of the definition of God as God is the greatest thing which can be conceived. This contradiction would be an absurd conclusion (*reductio ad absurdum*). Therefore, the opposite conclusion must be true. If God is the greatest thing which can be conceived then God must exist in both the understanding and in reality.

Anselm has faith in the existence of God and through logic has demonstrated that the opposite opinion, that God does not exist, would be absurd. Anselm has demonstrated:

> Therefore, Lord, not only are You that than which nothing greater can be conceived but You are also something greater than can be conceived. Indeed, since it is possible to be conceived to be something of this kind, if You are not this very thing, something can be conceived greater than You, which cannot be done.

Anselm, Proslogion 2, *1077–8*

The second part of Anselm's argument

So far, Anselm has suggested a proof for God's existence. However, for God to be God there must be more to Him than He simply exists (after all that would make God fundamentally similar to us). Anselm therefore develops his argument further and attempts to demonstrate that God's existence is **necessary**.

God's existence is necessary

To suggest that God is necessary is to suggest that there is no possibility of Him not existing. Anselm argues that we do know that God has necessary existence because:

- nothing greater than God can be conceived
- to be thought not to exist would be inferior to thinking of something that must always exist
- God must therefore necessarily exist.

Thus, Anselm argues that God exists because not only is God that than which nothing greater can be conceived, but also that God is a being with necessary existence.

> What art thou, then, Lord God, than whom nothing greater can be conceived?

Anselm, Proslogion 5, *1077–8*

Link

Look back to pvii in the Introduction and remind yourself of how *reductio ad absurdum* arguments establish their conclusions.

Think about

- Anselm's first argument is logical. Do you think it would persuade an atheist to believe in God?
- What are the reasons for your view?

Key terms

Necessary: by this, Anselm is referring to the eternal nature of God, and that God exists so truly that He cannot be thought of as not existing.

Explaining Anselm's ontological argument is not the same as simply outlining what he wrote. Trace each important step in the reasoning in order to give evidence of your understanding. Key terms and phrases that can be helpful here include: a priori; *reductio ad absurdum*; Anselm assumes; Anselm demonstrates (or shows); Anselm argues; and Anselm draws the conclusion that. Remember when answering questions relating to Anselm's version of the ontological argument that Anselm puts forward two arguments.

This is central to Anselm's argument as this is the difference between the fool and the believer. The fool knows the word 'God' but does not know God himself. It is only the believer who understands that because God is 'the greatest being that can be conceived', God cannot be thought of as not existing. If this is so then Anselm's conclusion, that those who doubt or deny the existence of God do not know what God is, remains and his argument that 'no one who understands what God is can conceive that God does not exist' stands.

Activities

1 Write a 500–600-word essay to explain Anselm's ontological argument.

2 Make a list of the strengths and weaknesses of Anselm's ontological argument.

3 Compare your list with the evaluation of other philosophers on pp7–16.

💡 Gaunilo's criticism of Anselm's ontological argument

A contemporary of Anselm, a Benedictine monk called Gaunilo of Marmoutiers, proposed a challenge to Anselm's ontological argument in his work *On behalf of the Fool*. He argued that simply because an atheist has understanding of the concept of God does not make the existence of God a reality.

> The fool might make this reply: This being is said to be in my understanding already, only because I understand what is said.

Gaunilo, On Behalf of the Fool

Gaunilo rejects that Anslem has proved the existence of God *reductio ad absurdum*, because he does not believe that Anselm's conclusion that because there is understanding of God as 'the greatest thing that can be conceived' means that God must exist in reality if valid. Gaunilo is arguing that we have understanding of many things, but it does not make them exist. The fact that an atheist such as the fool dismissed the existence of God demonstrates that there are different understandings of God. The very fact that he is arguing with Anselm as to whether the existence of God can be proved using the definition of God is evidence in itself that there is no common understanding of the meaning of the word 'God', and therefore the ontological argument cannot be used to support the existence of God.

The idea of a perfect island

Gaunilo criticises the process by which Anselm moves from his definition of God to his suggestion that God exists. Gaunilo stated that if someone were to describe to you a most perfect island, lost somewhere and basically untouched by man, and then state that it must exist because of its perfection, you would be a fool to believe him.

Gaunilo argues that we can think of a perfect island, but it does not make it exist.

> For example: it is said that somewhere in the ocean is an island, which, because of the difficulty, or rather the impossibility, of discovering what does not exist, is called the lost island. And they say that this island has an inestimable wealth of all manner of riches and delicacies in greater abundance than is told of the Islands

■ Think about

■ Anselm speaks of God as 'that than which nothing greater can be conceived'. Gaunilo, on the other hand, occupies himself with a comparison between islands, which can always be added to or changed because they are contingent whereas Anselm is referring to God who is perfect and cannot be changed. Therefore, Gaunilo's criticism is not valid in this context.

■ Who do you think is right: Anselm or Gaunilo?

of the Blest; and that having no owner or inhabitant, it is more excellent than all other countries, which are inhabited by mankind, in the abundance with which it is stored. Now if someone should tell me that there is such an island, I should easily understand his words, in which there is no difficulty. But suppose that he went on to say, as if by a logical inference: You can no longer doubt that this island which is more excellent than all the lands exists somewhere, since you have no doubt that it is in your understanding. And since it is more excellent not to be in understanding alone, but to exist both in the understanding and in reality, for this reason it must exist. For if it does not exist, any land which really exists will be more excellent than it; and so the island already understood by you to be more excellent will not be more excellent.

Gaunilo, On Behalf of the Fool

💡 Descartes' version of the ontological argument

René Descartes developed the ontological argument in ways that differ from Anselm's argument. Within his argument, Descartes still concentrates on the idea that the very fact that we have the concept of the God of classical theism must mean that God exists. As with Anselm's ontological argument, Descartes is putting forward an a priori argument.

Cogito ergo sum

René Descartes began by seeking to prove what we can be certain of in the universe, what we can know for sure. He concluded his own existence through his ability to think. This resulted in his famous saying, 'I think therefore I am' (*cogito ergo sum*). Descartes realised that although he could prove his own existence based on his own thoughts, he could not prove the existence of others. Having established that his thoughts were evidence of his own existence, Descartes went on to consider what else he could prove exists. He concluded that these included a priori things such as mathematics. He was aware of the properties of a triangle, and even if triangles had never existed they would still have the distinct characteristics of three sides and three angles. Descartes denies that he has come to know the nature of triangles through his senses as his senses would not derive the triangle's properties as clearly and distinctly as he does in his mind.

The first part of Descartes' argument

Having reasoned that a triangle must have all of the properties he ascribes to it because the triangle exists as an idea in his mind and he clearly and distinctly perceives all of its properties, Descartes develops the first part of his ontological argument. God exists as an idea in his mind. He had a clear and distinct definition of God as the 'supremely perfect being'.

But if the mere fact that I can produce from my thought the idea of something entails that everything which I clearly and distinctly perceive to belong to that thing really does belong to it, is not this a possible basis for another argument to prove the existence of God? Certainly, the idea of God, or a supremely perfect being, is one that I find within me just as surely as the idea of any shape or number. And my understanding that it belongs to his nature that he always exists is no less clear and distinct than is the case when I prove of any shape or number that some property belongs to its nature.

Descartes, Fifth Meditation, *1641*

Take it further

Read the whole of Gaunilo's argument, *On Behalf of the Fool*. You can find it at www.fordham.edu/halsall/basis/anselm-gaunilo.html.

Key philosopher

René Descartes (1596–1650)
He was a French philosopher important in this context for his version of the ontological argument.

Link

Look back at p1 to remind yourself of the attributes of the God of classical theism.

■ **Key terms**

Perfections: in the context of Descartes' ontological argument this means something that is flawless or lacking any faults.

Predicate: that part of a statement that makes an assertion about a subject – telling you what something is, does or has. The criticism is that the ontological argument incorrectly uses 'existence' as a property or quality that God possesses.

■ **Link**

Look back at p3 to remind yourself of the meaning of necessary existence when applied to God.

Descartes defined 'existence' as one of God's many **perfections**. Descartes is not relying on an arbitrary definition of God but on an innate idea of God that he believes people possess. Descartes is arguing that God's necessary existence is contained within our understanding of God as a 'supremely perfect being'. As imperfect beings, Descartes believes that humans cannot develop the idea of a perfect being themselves. Therefore, the idea must have come from the perfect being itself. Therefore, God exists.

> By the name God I understand a substance that is infinite (eternal, immutable), independent, all-knowing, all-powerful, and by which I myself and everything else, if anything else does exist, have been created. Now all these characteristics are such that the more diligently I attend to them, the less do they appear capable of proceeding from me alone; hence … we must conclude that God necessarily exists.

> *Descartes*, Fifth Meditation, *1641*

The second part of Descartes' argument

From God's necessary existence, Descartes develops the second part of his argument. Descartes is arguing that existence is a **predicate** of God because, as a most-perfect being, God must possess existence otherwise that being is not perfect. He believes we can conclude that God exists because existence is a predicate of a most-perfect being. The very essence of God includes existence. Therefore, God must exist in reality or God would not be perfect and this would be against the definition of God, which is absurd. Descartes says that trying to imagine God without the predicate of existence is illogical, like imagining a triangle without three sides or mountains without valleys!

> Existence is a part of the concept of a perfect being; anyone who denied that a perfect being had the property existence would be like someone who denied that a triangle had the property three-sidedness … the mind cannot conceive of triangularity without also conceiving of three-sidedness … the mind cannot conceive of perfection without also conceiving of existence.

> *Descartes*, Fifth Meditation, *1641*

Descartes' consideration of possible challenges to his argument

Descartes was aware that other philosophers would raise objections to his ontological argument, and he considered how to refute these possible objections.

Descartes begins with his argument that we cannot conceive of mountains without valleys, and considers the possible challenge that just because we have the concept of mountains and valleys does not mean that there are actual valleys and mountains. In response to this possible challenge to his argument, Descartes agrees that all that can be said is if there are mountains then there are valleys, but the same is not true when referring to God. The concept of God means that God exists. Descartes continues by agreeing with Anselm that the argument only applies to God because God is the only supremely perfect being from whom we are entitled to infer existence.

> But the cases are not analogous, and a fallacy lurks under the semblance of this objection: for because I cannot conceive a mountain without a valley, it does not follow that there is any mountain or valley in existence, but simply that the mountain or

■ **Take it further**

Read Descartes' version of the ontological argument in the *Fifth Meditation*.

■ **Activity**

Write a 500–600-word essay to explain Descartes' ontological argument.

valley, whether they do or do not exist, are inseparable from each other; whereas, on the other hand, because I cannot conceive God unless as existing, it follows that existence is inseparable from him, and therefore that he really exists: not that this is brought about by my thought, or that it imposes any necessity on things, but, on the contrary, the necessity which lies in the thing itself, that is, the necessity of the existence of God.

Descartes, Fifth Meditation, *1641*

ⓘ Key objections to the ontological argument

The main objections to the ontological argument are based on:

- the definition of God
- existence as a predicate of God
- the possibility of deriving existence claims from definition.

Objections based on the definition of God

Aquinas' challenge

St Thomas Aquinas' (1224–74) challenges to Anselm would also apply to Descartes' version of the ontological argument. Aquinas rejects that there can be certainty that the human mind has the correct concept of God. He argues that God is beyond human understanding; therefore, humans cannot prove that God exists from their mere idea of God. The existence of God is not self-evident.

> The proposition 'God exists' is self-evident to God. For God knows he is the eternally existent Perfect Being. God knows the meaning of the term 'God' by direct self-awareness. Hence God knows that eternal existence belongs to Himself. However, the proposition 'God exists' is not self-evident to the human mind. For the human mind does not have an intuition of the essence of God. The human mind can make up a definition of the term 'God'; and we can say that if that definition is correct, then God necessarily exists. However, the question is: Do we have a correct definition of the term 'God'?

Aquinas, Summa Theologica, *1265–74*

Aquinas continues that even if we have an inborn idea of God, it is confused:

> To know that God exists in a general and indefinite way is implanted in us by nature, inasmuch as God is man's beatitude. For man naturally desires happiness, and what is naturally desired by a man must be naturally known to him. This, however, is not to know absolutely that God exists; as to know that someone is approaching is not the same as to know that Peter is approaching, even though it is Peter who is approaching; for there are many who imagine that man's perfect good (which is happiness) consists in riches, and others in pleasures, and others something else.

Aquinas, Summa Theologica, *1265–74*

Examiner's tip

Remember when answering questions related to Descartes' version of the ontological argument that Descartes puts forward two arguments.

■ Link

Look back at p vi–vii in the Introduction and remind yourself of what is meant by an a priori and an a posteriori argument.

■ Take it further

Using the internet and/or library, find out more about Thomas Aquinas.

■ Link

Read Chapter 2, pp 30–31 to find out how St Thomas Aquinas thought that it was possible to talk about God.

Is the complex design of the human body evidence for the existence of God?

In Aquinas' view, we cannot come to know God as He is beyond human understanding, and therefore a priori arguments to prove the existence of God fail as we cannot define God. We can only know that God exists through the effects of God's work in the world, such as the evidence of design in nature. Other philosophers agree that it is not possible from a definition of the word 'God' to prove that God exists.

Aquinas' point that humans cannot understand God is answered if the view that Anselm's *Proslogion* is a prayer to God to aid faith rather than an argument for the existence of God, is accepted.

David Hume's criticisms

David Hume raised objections to the ontological argument that are essentially twofold:

1 He argued that it is not possible to take an idea in one's mind, apply pure logic to that idea, and reach a conclusion based entirely in the external, observable universe.

2 He argued (like Kant later) that existence cannot be treated as a predicate which something can 'have' or 'not have', or which can be added to or subtracted from something.

In response to Hume's first objection, some would say that as human beings, we base our lives around that which we can observe rather than that which we can rationally prove. If this is the case, then Hume's argument is fairly robust and it has grounds for rejecting most forms of the argument. But is this the case?

Hume's second objection challenges the view that existence can be something which, when added to the definition of X, actually changes X. He said:

> The idea of existence, then, is the very same with the idea of what we conceive to be existent. To reflect on any thing simply, and to reflect on it as existent, are nothing different from each other. That idea, when conjoined with the idea of any object, makes no addition to it. Whatever we conceive, we conceive to be existent.

David Hume, Treatise on Human Nature, *1739*

In other words, to think of God as 'in the mind' and then to think of God as 'in reality' is, according to Hume, exactly the same thing. Combining this idea with the first part of his objection, we could suggest that all we are doing is 'thinking about God' and not providing grounds for His existence.

💡 Objections based on the use of existence as a predicate

Kant's criticisms

In many ways, Kant built on and developed the criticism put forward by David Hume. Kant criticised Descartes' claim that existence is a property of perfection and that existence is a predicate. Kant objects to Descartes' claim that denying God's existence is tantamount to denying that triangles have three sides, which is contradictory. He states that if we dismisses the idea of both the three sides (predicate) and the idea of the triangle itself (subject); there is no contradiction. It is therefore possible to dismiss the concept of God.

Kant argues that according to Descartes we can define a thing as we see fit, but whether or not anything matches that definition in reality is another question altogether. Therefore, it would seem that Kant has dealt with Descartes' notion of existence as a predicate.

Kant raises a second objection that 'existence is not a predicate'. This means that saying 'X exists' tells us nothing about X (whereas 'X is female' or 'X is tall' does). He said:

> By whatever predicates we may conceive of a thing we do not make the least addition to the thing when we further declare that the thing is.

Kant, Critique of Pure Reason, *1781*

Kant states that a predicate must give us information about X; 'X is' does not. In fact the opposite statement presents us with a **paradox**: if 'X exists' tells us about a property that X has, then 'X does not exist' denies that it has this property (or affirms that it lacks it). But, how can that which does not exist lack anything?

Existence as a synthetic proposition

Kant also claimed that God cannot be placed in a separate category to everything else, and in doing so Anselm and Descartes had given a synthetic proposition the status of an analytic proposition and broken the rules of grammar.

In an analytic proposition the assertion about the subject is contained within the subject definition, for example a square is a four-sided figure with equal sides. To suggest that a square is anything other than a four-sided figure with equal sides would be illogical as the definition of a square is known a priori.

> The word *reality* in the conception of the thing, and the word *existence* in the conception of the predicate, will not help you out of the difficulty. For, supposing you were to term all positing of a thing reality, you have thereby posited the thing with all its predicates in the conception of the subject and assumed its actual existence, and this you merely repeat in the predicate. But if you confess, as every reasonable person must, that every existential proposition is synthetical, how can it be maintained that the predicate of existence cannot be denied without contradiction? – a property which is the characteristic of analytical propositions, alone.

Kant, Critique of Pure Reason, *1788*

Key philosopher

Immanuel Kant (1724–1804)
He was a German philosopher who wrote *Critique of Pure Reason*.

AQA Examiner's tip

The AQA specification uses a range of technical terms. Expect those terms to be used in the questions set. For this topic we have 'existence as a predicate of God', 'the possibility of deriving existential claims from definition' and 'proof'.

Links

■ Look back to p6 to remind yourself of the meaning of the term predicate.

■ Look back at pviii in the Introduction to remind yourself of what is meant by synthetic and analytic propositions.

Key terms

Paradox: a statement that seems absurd or contradictory even if the statement appears well founded.

Think about

Is Kant right in arguing that you can dismiss the idea of God? What evidence could you produce to support your answer?

Take it further

Read Kant's arguments for rejecting the ontological argument in *Critique of Pure Reason*.

Key philosopher

Bertrand Russell (1872–1970)
He was a leading 20th-century philosopher. His *History of Western Philosophy* (1945) became a bestseller.

Key terms

Syllogism: a form of deductive reasoning where the argument moves from the general to the specific to reach a conclusion. For example:

- All humans are mortal.
- I am human.
- Therefore I am mortal.

Kant argues that it is not possible to include existence within an analytical proposition as it is always possible to contradict existence as a property of a thing. Propositions related to existence are therefore synthetic as it is necessary to prove the existence of things using evidence (a posteriori). It is therefore a synthetic proposition to state that God exists.

The meaning of 'exist'

Bertrand Russell claimed that the ontological argument uses the word 'exist' incorrectly. Existence cannot be a predicate. If it were, we could construct the following **syllogism**:

- Men exist in the world.
- Santa Claus is a man.
- Therefore, Santa Claus exists.

'Of course I exist!'

This syllogism appears a valid argument and yet we know that the conclusion that Santa Claus exists is wrong. This false conclusion is reached because of the misuse of 'man' in the second predicate. Santa Claus is a fictional male character and belongs in a different category to the men referred to in the first predicate. It is therefore inaccurate to make the jump to the conclusion that as men exist in this world, Santa Claus must exist. Russell's argument is that existence is not a property of things, but of the idea of those things.

Russell used the example of dragons. We have the idea of what the word 'dragon' means. However, when people say, 'Dragons do not exist', it means of all the things that exist, the word 'dragon' refers to none of them. When I say, 'A cow is a quadruped with udders, etc.', my intention is to describe a cow. The fact that a cow exists provides an extension to my description but it is not part of the description. Therefore, existence is an extension of an intention. When we conceive of a cow, it is easy to accept its existence as we see cows in fields. We can say the same for most 'things' experienced, but the same is not true of God.

Intention and extension

Russell has put the ontological argument into different terms. He states that labelling and defining something is to provide an intention (description) concerning the object under discussion. Russell concludes that 'that than which nothing greater can be conceived' is simply the totality of everything that can be conceived by the human mind related to the idea of God. That is the intention of the phrase, but does it have an extension?

The answer according to Russell would be that 'that than which nothing greater can be conceived' exists in the understanding as the totality of all ideas about God. Nevertheless, those ideas do not have to have physical existence, and there is no evidence to prove the existence. Russell would support Anselm's claim that God is the greatest thing we can think of, but not Anselm's belief that this proves God's existence in reality. For Russell there is a difference between understanding something and experiencing something. Therefore, for Russell the argument does not prove the existence of God and does not challenge disbelief in God.

Activity

Write a response to the following statement: 'The criticisms presented by Gaunilo and Russell successfully reject Anselm's arguments.' Discuss.

First- and second-order predicates

Gottlob Frege (1848–1925) distinguishes between first-order predicates and second-order predicates. First-order predicates tell us something about the nature of concepts and apply directly to objects themselves. For example, 'John's horses are brown' or, 'All cats are mammals'. First-order predicates provide information about the relation of two concepts. For example, whatever falls under the concept of a cat is a mammal. Whatever falls under the concept of the horses owned by John is brown. However, one concept is not a property of the other. Being a mammal is not a property of the concept of being a cat, and being brown is not a property of the concept of a horse but rather, of the objects falling under that concept, just as being a cat or a horse itself is. Hence, the two concepts are of the same logical order and they both apply to objects.

The second-order predicates apply only to first-order concepts and not to objects themselves. Second-order predicates do not apply to objects but tell us about concepts of the first order. 'Exist' can only be applied as a second-order predicate. For example, the statements 'mammals exist', 'cats exist' and 'horses exist' are not about any particular mammal, cat or horse but rather about the concepts of mammals, cats and horses.

Frege concludes that existence is not a first-order predicate, as it does not tell us about the nature of something. Existence as a second-order predicate does not add to our understanding of the concept. Therefore, Frege concludes that existence cannot be used as a predicate to prove the existence of God.

Activity

Try to come up with your own examples of first-order and second-order predicates. Assess how and what each predicate tells you about the subject it is referring to.

Think about

- What about my intention of a unicorn, that it is 'a quadruped with one horn'. Is there a problem when I add (extend) existence to my intention?
- If so what is the problem?

Objections based on the possibility of deriving existence claims from definition

The meaning of 'is'

The philosopher Brian Davies recognises attempts by philosophers such as Norman Malcolm to distinguish between existence and necessity but criticises his use of the word 'is'. Davies illustrates this point using the concept of a pixie. 'A pixie is a little man with pointed ears. Therefore, there actually exists a pixie.' He goes on to suggest that if we were to claim that the pixie must exist in order to have those pointed ears, we would surely find the reasoning unacceptable.

Davies states that the word 'is' can be used in two different ways:

- It can be used to define something: 'A queen is a female monarch'.
- It can explain that there actually is something, for example, 'There is such a thing as a vampire'.

Davies suggests that the first use says nothing about existence, in that it says nothing about an existent queen. However, the statement does explain what the word 'queen' means.

The second use, on the other hand, whilst also saying nothing about existence, is not defining anything either. It is saying that a vampire is, and by this statement implicitly supposing its existence.

From this, we can conclude that Malcolm's argument favours moving from the premise, 'A pixie is a little man with pointed ears' (an example of the first use) as a definition, to the conclusion, 'Pixies actually exist' (an example from the second use). What Davies argues is that Malcolm's error is to go from the definition of God as a being with necessary existence, to explain that there is a being with necessary existence. The ontological argument may help us to have a definition of God but it does not prove that the being with this definition exists.

■ Responses to the objections

In recent times, the ontological argument has had support from modern philosophers who consider that it is still a valid argument to prove the existence of God. Philosophers such as Norman Malcolm and Alvin Plantinga disagree with the objections of Russell and Davies. They consider that the fact that the ontological argument is an a priori argument based on an agreed understanding of the definition of the word 'God' makes it a logical argument to prove God's existence.

A development of the necessary existence of God

Norman Malcolm (1911–90) considered Anselm's arguments and concluded he could not support Anselm's first argument because it is not valid, as existence is not a characteristic. However, Malcolm supported Anselm's second argument because:

- The concept of God is the concept of a being whose existence is necessary.
- It is not possible to think of a being that necessarily exists not existing.
- Therefore, Malcolm argues, God must exist.

Activities

1 Make your own list of examples of the two ways in which, according to Davies, the word 'is' may be used.

2 Do you think Davies' argument is valid? Explain the reasons for your answer.

3 How does your conclusion relate to Malcolm's version of the ontological argument?

To support this conclusion, Malcolm develops Anselm's second argument as follows:

> If God, a being greater than which cannot be conceived, does not exist then he cannot come into existence. For if He did He would either have been caused to come into existence or have happened to come into existence, and in either case He would be a limited being, which by our conception of Him He is not. Since He cannot come into existence, if He does not exist His existence is impossible. If He does exist He cannot have come into existence … nor can He cease to exist, for nothing could cause Him to cease to exist nor could it just happen that He ceased to exist. So if God exists His existence is necessary. Thus God's existence is either impossible or necessary. It can be the former only if the concept of such a being is self-contradictory or in some way logically absurd. Assuming that this is not so, it follows that He necessarily exists.

Norman Malcolm in John Hick (ed.), The Existence of God, 1982

Possible worlds

Alvin Plantinga (1932–) developed the philosophical notion of **possible worlds**. For example, in our world, John F. Kennedy was an American president. However, this was not necessarily so; he could have made a different career choice and been an estate agent! This is an example of two different possible worlds – one in which JFK was an American president and was assassinated and another in which he was an estate agent who lived to be 90 years old.

In each of the possible worlds you have considered above, there will be many differences. That is the whole point of this philosophical notion: the possibilities are **infinite**.

An estate agent?!

Think about

- If something caused God to come into existence, or God *happened* to come into existence, why would God be a *limited* being?
- Is it acceptable and coherent to conclude that God exists because God has the property of necessary existence?
- What are the reasons for your answer?

Key terms

Possible worlds: a complete way that things could be. It is not another world (that is, a physical earth floating a long time ago, in a galaxy far, far away!).

Infinite: boundless or endless.

Activity

Based on the definition of possible worlds, consider your own position in, say, three years time. Write down how you think your life will differ if you are:

- at university
- unemployed
- celebrating a lottery win
- suffering with a terminal illness.

Each of these scenarios is part of a possible world.

■ Link

Look back to p1 to remind yourself of the attributes of the God of classical theism.

■ Think about

■ Consider Plantinga's claim that since there is a possible world where a being with maximal excellence exists, we therefore actually have such a being in our world.

■ Do you consider this coherent?

■ What are the reasons for your opinion?

Why does Plantinga consider Gaunilo's challenge to Anselm fails?

■ Key terms

Contingent: to be dependent on other events or circumstances for existence so that it might occur or might not occur. Humans are contingent beings, as is everything within the universe. Many philosophers argue that the universe itself is contingent.

■ Activity

Write a 500–600-word essay explaining Plantinga's version of the ontological argument.

Maximal greatness and maximal existence

With this in mind, Plantinga offers a description of another possible world:

■ There is a possible world, W, in which there exists a being with 'maximal greatness'.

■ A being has maximal greatness only if it exists in every possible world.

This means that in every possible world that we envisage, there is a being of 'maximal greatness'. However, this does not mean God, for Plantinga states that to be maximally great a being only has to be present in every possible world. He has not, as yet, demonstrated that this being is the omnipotent God of classical theism. Indeed it would be possible that in each world there may be an individual being that is more powerful, more knowing, more morally perfect etc. than this maximally great being. It is irrelevant even if each of these beings are found only in one possible world.

To deal with this, Plantinga introduces the concept of 'maximal excellence'.

He states that:

■ Maximal greatness entails maximal excellence.

■ Maximal excellence entails omnipotence, omniscience and moral perfection.

Therefore:

■ There is a possible world in which there is a being that is maximally great.

■ If maximally great, this being exists in our world.

■ This being has maximal excellence, as this is entailed within maximal greatness.

■ This means that there is an omnipotent, omniscient and morally perfect being in *our* world.

■ Therefore, there *is* a God.

According to Davies, even if we accept that a being with maximal excellence is possible, and therefore it is possible that such a being exists in our world, it does not follow that such a being actually exists. All that we can coherently conclude from Plantinga's evidence is that maximal excellence is possible, and therefore God is possible, not actual.

Plantinga referred back to Gaunilo's use of islands to challenge Anselm, and pointed out that islands are **contingent** whereas God is eternal. Also, islands do not have 'intrinsic maximum'.

> The qualities that make for greatness in islands – numbers of palm trees, amount and quality of coconuts, for example – most of these qualities have no intrinsic maximum. That is there is no degree of productivity or number of palm tree … such that it is impossible that an island display more of that quality. So the idea of a greatest possible island is an inconsistent or an incoherent idea; it's not possible that there be such a thing. And hence the analogue of step (3) of Anselm's argument (it is possible that God exists) is not true for the perfect island argument: so that argument fails.

Alvin Plantinga, The Analytic Theist: An Alvin Plantinga Reader, *1998*

Whether existence is a property

Charles Hartshorne (1897–2000) argues that philosophers ignore one aspect of Anselm's argument. Hartshorne considers that Anselm uses existence differently in his two arguments. He agrees that existence is not always a **property** of something, but continues by adding that this does not mean that existence is never a property. For Hartshorne, when applied to the necessary existence of God it is a property. The fact that God has necessary existence and is not contingent means that God is greater than contingent beings. If to have necessary existence a being must always exist then it is logically impossible for God not to exist. Therefore, the conclusion must be that God exists.

What philosophers such as Hartshorne and Malcolm are arguing is that if God has to have necessary existence to be God then it is a contradiction to say that God does not exist.

The meaning of necessary existence

John Hick considers that Anselm was not using the modern understanding of necessary existence but the medieval understanding that God is a necessary being that is dependent on no other being for existence, and whose existence has no beginning or end. However, even with this different understanding of necessary existence, God would have to exist or the understanding of what we mean by God would have to change.

💡 Significance of the ontological argument for faith

Many philosophers respond to the various criticisms by arguing that the ontological argument does not go beyond defining God. It helps people to consider the attributes of the God of classical theism, but having an understanding of the definition of God does not convince atheists or agnostics of the existence of God. Whether or not people believe in the existence of God probably depends more on **faith** than their understanding of the word God.

An argument against the ontological argument is that it is possible to think of the non-existence of God. Gaunilo's argument on behalf of the fool demonstrates that an atheist can have understanding of the word God, but then not have faith in the existence of such a being in reality. Anselm, on the other hand, would say that the argument is seeking to take people beyond the definition of the word 'God' to knowledge of God, Himself. If Anselm is right then the ontological argument could be an aid to faith.

The relationship between faith and reason

One significance of the ontological argument for faith is whether or not the argument presents valid reasons for believing in God's existence. This raises the question as to whether faith is grounded in reason or reason is governed by faith. Anselm himself recognised the relationship between faith and reason and how they aid each other in understanding the nature of God. Anselm considered that reason alone can lead to error and therefore it has to be supported by faith as it is only through faith that greater understanding can be achieved.

> Nor do I seek to understand so that I can believe (intelligere ut credam), but rather I believe so that I can understand (credo ut intelligam). For I believe this too, that 'unless I believe I shall not understand'.

Anselm, Proslogion 1, *1077–8*

■ Links

- ■ Look back at p15 to be sure that you understand what is meant by faith.
- ■ Look back to p vii in the Introduction and remind yourself of what is meant by a valid and good argument.

■ Activity

Write a definition of the God of classical theism.

Anselm already accepts the existence of God and is not providing a logical argument that will convince people to believe in God. However, the ontological argument does appeal to reason and its logic is very convincing. Even Russell himself accepted the logic of the ontological argument:

> I had gone out to buy a tin of tobacco, and was going back with it along Trinity Lane, when I suddenly threw it up in the air and exclaimed: 'Great God in Boots! – the ontological argument is sound!'

Russell, Autobiography of Bertrand Russell, *Vol. 1, 1967*

Russell is saying that through logical reasoning it appears that a being with necessary existence must exist, but when we consider the argument further, merely having the definition does not make God exist.

As Kant stated with regard to Descartes' version of the ontological argument:

> To posit a triangle, and yet to reject its three angles, is self-contradictory; but there is no self-contradiction in rejecting the triangle altogether with its three angles. The same holds true of the concept of an absolutely necessary being.

Kant, Critique of Pure Reason, *1788*

If the believer accepts that there is a God, then the ontological argument may be a valid argument that God's existence is necessary. In the same way that if there is a triangle it must have three sides, for a believer who believes that they understand the concept of God then for them God exists. The significance of the argument for faith is that it might help to develop a believer's understanding of God. This could conceivably strengthen a person's relationship with God, perhaps giving further reason to praise God's nature. The success or failure of the argument as a proof of God's existence, however, would have very limited significance for the overall faith of a believer. If successful, it would only provide an alternative way of confirming faith. Its failure, therefore, would do nothing to take away faith.

By definition, therefore, God is theoretically possible. However, having the concept does not make God a reality for agnostics and atheists. Many commentators conclude that the ontological argument works only for someone who already has some sort of faith and the argument is unlikely to persuade agnostics and atheists that God exists as their understanding of the concept of God is different from the believer's. Non-believers would not accept that belief in God as a perfect being leads to the valid conclusion that God exists. Philosophers such as Kant and Russell did not believe that it is a good argument as there is a misuse of 'existence' as a predicate. They would question the validity of statements such as 'God must exist because he is a supremely perfect being', and consider it to be a misleading argument.

Therefore, the argument only works for believers such as Anselm who hold as a matter of faith that God exists. For the believer it is a deductive argument that reaches the reasoned conclusion that they already held, through faith, that God exists.

Faith may be the only proof

Karl Barth (1886–1968) denied the possibility of attaining any knowledge of God through the use of reason. Barth considered the ontological argument in light of its relationship between faith and reason in his work, *Fides Quaerens Intellectu* (Faith Seeking Understanding). Barth is a supporter of the view that Anselm's intention was not to prove the existence of God to the fool (atheist) but to offer a prayer of meditation on God as the Supreme Being in whom he has faith. Barth points out that it is this very fact, that the *Proslogion* is a prayer addressed to God, that the critics of Anselm miss.

Barth argues that Anselm's definition of God as 'something than which nothing greater can be conceived' is not presented as the beginning of an argument for the existence of God but as a description by a believer of what is understood about God within the limits of the human mind. Barth points out that if humans had the mental capacity to understand God and to prove God's existence then it would not be necessary to have faith in God's self-revelation of His existence to them.

Barth also considers Anselm's assertion that God has necessary existence to be a statement of faith as without the existence of God then humans and the world in which they live would not exist.

Barth's arguments in relation to Anselm's ontological argument cannot be applied to Descartes' version of the argument as Descartes was seeking to present an argument using reason to prove the existence of God.

Could the ontological argument weaken faith?

One unusual response to this view would be that the success of the argument could actually be damaging to faith. This view could be adopted by those who consider that an essential element of faith is that it is based on belief rather than proven fact. The point would be that if God's existence could be proved conclusively then the element of faith, upon which religion is based, would be redundant, which would require a major re-evaluation of the relationship between God and humans.

Religious believers who are anti-realists would give a different response.

Anti-realism is a theory of truth. It holds that the truth or falsity of a statement depends not on whether it corresponds to the objective reality of what it describes, but on whether it corresponds to the situation, as a person understands it. For example, whether God exists does not depend on whether there is or is not an objectively existing omnipotent being, but on whether we understand there to be such a being – which, of course, depends on which person we ask. Upon this view, religious believers are right to say that 'God exists', for He does truly exist as a concept within the religious community.

For anti-realists, the ontological argument has extra force. For members of a religious community that accepts the existence of God, the statement 'God necessarily exists' is true by definition. Merely to believe in God guarantees that God exists.

This view lends an extra dimension of support to Anselm's argument. If the statement, 'God is that than which nothing greater can be conceived' is uttered prayerfully to God by a religious believer, then we can say by definition that such a God exists. Given that a believer, as part of a prayer, wrote Anselm's argument to God, its success at this level is clear. Of course what the ontological argument cannot do is tell us whether this definition of God corresponds to any objective reality beyond the mind of the believer(s).

Take it further

Read Karl Barth's monograph, *Fides Quaerens Intellectum*.

Key terms

Anti-realism: in philosophy, the term describes any position involving either the denial of the objective reality of entities of a certain type or the denial that verification-transcendent statements about a type of entity are either true or false.

Take it further

Using the internet and/or library find out more about the philosophical understanding of anti-realism.

Link

Look back to p vii in the Introduction and remind yourself how using *reductio ad absurdum* proves arguments.

Failure of the argument to strengthen faith

As we have seen, many philosophers consider that the ontological argument will strengthen the faith of those who already believe in God and is as Anselm states, an aid to 'faith seeking understanding'.

However, for those who do not believe in God it appears to be an argument that will not convert an atheist into faith in God. Such a view is presented by Richard Dawkins (1941–) in *The God Delusion*. Dawkins concludes that as the ontological argument does not prove the existence of God, it has no significance for faith:

> Kant identified the trick card up Anselm's sleeve as his slippery assumption that 'existence' is more 'perfect' than non-existence. The American philosopher, Norman Malcolm, put it like this: 'The doctrine that existence is a perfection is remarkably queer. It makes sense and is true to say my future house will be a better one if it is insulated than if it is not insulated; but what could it mean to say that it will be a better house if it exists than it does not?' Another philosopher, the Australian Douglas Gasking, made the point with his ironic 'proof' that God does not exist (Anselm's contemporary Gaunilo had suggested a somewhat similar *reductio*).
>
> 1 The creation of the world is the most marvellous achievement imaginable.
>
> 2 The merit of an achievement is the product of (a) its intrinsic quality, and (b) the ability of its creator.
>
> 3 The greater the disability (or handicap) of the creator, the more impressive the achievement.
>
> 4 The most formidable handicap for a creator would be non-existence.
>
> 5 Therefore if we suppose that the universe is the product of an existent creator we can conceive a greater being – namely, one who created everything while not existing.
>
> 6 An existing God therefore would not be a being greater than which a greater cannot be conceived because an even more formidable and incredible creator would be a God which did not exist. Ergo:
>
> 7 God does not exist.

Richard Dawkins, The God Delusion, *2006*

Think about

■ Do you think Gasking's argument that a non-existent being could create everything is a logical argument?

■ Does Gasking's argument undermine Anselm's concept of God?

Gasking is demonstrating that it is possible to think of a being that is even more powerful that one with necessary existence, which does not exist and yet created everything. This may seem an absurd suggestion but it is demonstrating that there can be different concepts of 'that than which nothing greater can be conceived'.

Dawkins concludes:

> Gasking didn't really prove that God does not exist.
>
> By the same token, Anselm didn't prove that he does.

Richard Dawkins, The God Delusion, *2006*

Conclusion

Whether the ontological argument has any significance for faith is therefore controversial. By considering the definition of the God of classical theism, it helps to establish what the monotheistic religions say about God. It helps to establish that God is omniscient, omnipotent, benevolent and transcendent; God is the summary of all perfection.

The ontological argument does establish that the relationship between God and humans is more dependent on faith. It is therefore an argument that is more an aid to those who already have faith than proving the existence of God to those who have not. Anselm himself describes the ontological argument as 'faith seeking understanding'. It may be that we can only know of God what God chooses to reveal of Himself, and this may mean that we do not have an adequate understanding of God to prove His existence. Faith may be the only proof. Moojan Momen concludes that believers may argue:

> Our religion is only true religion, they assert, if it is based on faith, not on reason and human intellect. This reaction can be found historically in the Protestant 'dialectical theology' of such figures as Karl Barth, produced in reaction to the Catholic 'natural theology' of Aquinas and Anselm; and also the Ash'ari reaction to the rationalist theology of Mu'tazila in medieval Islam.

Moojan Momen, The Phenomenon of Religion: A Thematic Approach, *1999*

Activities

1. Use the internet to find out what is meant by 'dialectical theology', 'natural theology' and 'rationalist theology of Mu'tazila'.

2. Write your own definition of each theology.

3. Do you agree with Momen's conclusion? Give reasons for your opinion.

Further reading and weblinks

Charlesworth, M. (ed.) *St Anselm's Proslogion, with A Reply on Behalf of the Fool by Gaunilo and The Author's Reply to Gaunilo*, University of Notre Dame Press, 1979. A consideration of the original debate between Anselm and Gaunilo.

Dawkins, R. *The God Delusion*, Bantam Press, 2006. The book presents Dawkins' reasons for rejecting the existence of God.

Descartes' *Meditations* Ontological Argument, www.infidels.org/library/modern/james_still/descartes.html. James Still considers Descartes' ontological argument supported by quotes from Descartes' *Fifth Meditation*.

Hick, John H. *Philosophy of Religion*, Prentice Hall, 1990. Chapter 2 begins with a consideration of the strengths and weaknesses of the ontological argument.

Jackson, R. 'The God of Philosophy', *TPM* (*The Philosopher's Magazine*), 2001. Chapter 4 considers Anselm's first and second ontological arguments, modern supporters and critics of the argument, the modal ontological argument and how the argument may or may not help the understanding of God.

Malcolm, N. 'Anselm's Ontological Argument' in *The Existence of God (Problems of Philosophy)*, Macmillan, 1982. Norman Malcolm explains why he cannot support Anselm's first argument but considers that the second argument of Anselm is valid.

Medieval Sourcebook: Anselm on God's Existence, www.fordham.edu/halsall/source/anselm.html. This site has excerpts from the Proslogion, Gaunilo's Response, and Anselm's Reply, plus some commentary by David Burr on the ontological argument.

Plantinga, A. *The Ontological Argument from St Anselm to Contemporary Philosophers*, Doubleday, 1965. Plantinga explains why the ontological argument proves the existence of God.

Vogel Carey, T. 'The Ontological Argument and the Sin of Hubris', *Philosophy Now*, 53, 24–27. Vogel examines aspects of the ontological argument.

The Internet Encyclopedia of Philosophy: The Ontological Argument, www.iep.utm.edu/o/ont-arg.htm. This covers all of the major issues related to the ontological argument including the different forms of the arguments and the challenges to the argument.

Now that you have read this chapter, you should be able to:

■ summarise the ontological argument as presented by Anselm and Descartes

■ evaluate the strengths and weaknesses of the argument

■ evaluate how far the argument makes it reasonable for a non-believer to believe in God

■ assess the relationship between faith and reason as reflected in the ontological argument

■ assess the significance of the success or failure of the argument for faith.

2 Religious language

Learning objectives:

■ to understand the problem of the meaningfulness of religious language

■ to understand the verification principle

■ to understand the responses to the verification principle

■ to understand the different views of religious language

■ to evaluate the different views of religious language

■ to evaluate how successfully religion has responded to the challenge of the verification principle

■ to evaluate how successful are the various explanations of the nature of religious language

■ to assess whether it is possible to talk meaningfully about God.

■ Link

Look back at the attributes of the God of classical theism on p1 of Chapter 1 and Descartes' definition of God on p6.

■ Key terms

Meaningfulness: making sense.

Cognitive: when applied to religious language, this communicates knowledge, information and facts about God.

Anthropomorphises: attributes human form or personality to a god, animal or object.

■ The problem of religious language

An issue that dominated the discussion of the philosophy of religion during much of the 20th century centred on the **meaningfulness** of religious language. Religious language is the communication of ideas about God, faith, belief and practice. The problem with the communication of these ideas is that behind the words used are concepts. Individuals have different understandings of the concepts and this might result in differences of interpretation and meaning. Some philosophers argue that religious language is used in different ways from everyday language. It could show someone's commitment to a particular faith tradition, or make a claim on behalf of that tradition.

Some assert that religious language is **cognitive** and therefore something about God may be known. The problem with this is that religious statements are not about objective facts that can be proved true or false. The argument put forward is that if we are unable to validate religious statements based on objective facts that are open to cognition then religious language is considered to be meaningless.

There is the problem of how God is to be described when nothing is known about God. For example, is it right to refer to a supreme being using human terminology such as 'He' and 'Him' or referring to what God 'said'? It is felt that the use of language in this way **anthropomorphises** or objectifies God. Using words in this way appears to limit God's majesty or power in some way.

This has led to religious believers seeking ways in which they can talk about God in a meaningful way and some non-believers seeking to demonstrate why religious language is meaningless. One such group of philosophers who considered religious language as meaningless was the logical positivists.

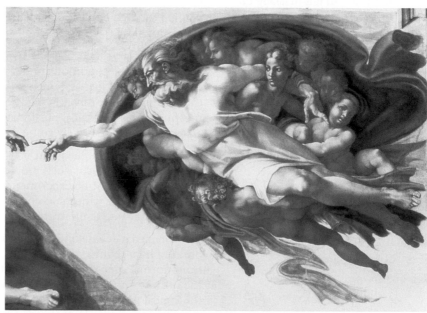

It is felt by some that referring to God as 'he' or 'him' anthropomorphises God, just as Michelangelo's depiction of God does on the Sistine Chapel ceiling

■ **Key terms**

Verification: the ascertainment of the truth of something. It means to prove that an assertion is either true or false.

The verification principle: the idea that the meaning of a statement lies in the method of its verification – and so that any statement that cannot be verified, even if only in theory, is meaningless. The principle is associated with the logical positivists and their attack on the meaningfulness of religious language.

■ **Think about**

Why do you think that the logical positivists would reject the ontological argument?

■ **Activities**

1 The logical positivists were not concerned with whether a proposition is true or false but whether or not it makes sense. They argued that if you do not know how to verify a proposition then it cannot have meaning. For example, 'all elephants are small' is not true, but it is meaningful because it can be verified.

2 Make your own list of statements that are meaningful because they can be verified.

3 Make a list of statements that the logical positivists would consider meaningless because they cannot be verified.

■ Link

Look back at pp vi–vii of the Introduction. What is the difference between an a priori argument and an a posteriori argument?

■ **Activity**

Find out what it means to verify things empirically. Discover examples of things proved true or false using empirical evidence.

💡 The logical positivists

The logical positivists developed from the work of philosophers known as the Vienna Circle. The circle was a group of philosophers working in Vienna in the 1920s, and included Moriz Schlick and Rudolf Carnap. The philosophical group did not seek to understand how we gain knowledge of the external world, but how we use language as the means of conveying knowledge. The fundamental principle of Logical Positivism was that only those propositions which can be verified empirically (or logically, in the case of analytical statements) have meaning. As the leader of the Vienna Circle put it: 'The meaning of a proposition is the method of **verification**' (Moritz Schlick (1882–1936)).

The logical positivists only accepted two forms of verifiable language.

■ Analytic propositions (a priori) – by which knowledge is gained through logical reasoning. These are propositions that are true by definition, for example 'all bachelors are unmarried'. We know this proposition is true because bachelor *means* an unmarried man. It would be a contradiction to deny an analytical truth – to refer to a 'married bachelor', for example.

■ Synthetic propositions (a posteriori) – by which knowledge could be proved true or false (verified) by some form of sense experience or experiment. For example, the statement 'John is a bachelor' could be verified by discovering whether or not John is male and unmarried.

💡 *The verification principle*

The theory developed by the logical positivists is known as **the verification principle**. The principle is stating *that we know the meaning of a statement if we know the conditions under which the statement is true or false*. If it is not possible to know how to prove the statement true or false, using either knowledge gained through logical reasoning or verified through empirical evidence, then the logical positivists regard it as meaningless.

Remember that the logical positivists accepted statements as meaningful if they knew the conditions under which the statement could be proved true or false, not just statements that could be proved true. For example, the statement 'the moon is made of green cheese' is false. It would be meaningful to the logical positivists as it is known how to prove the statement false: that is by going to the moon and taking rock samples.

Logical positivists argued that it was pointless to talk about God, ethics, art and metaphysics as such propositions could not be verified using the senses or scientific experiment. It was not possible to know the conditions under which such propositions could be proved true or false and therefore such talk must be meaningless.

This opened a debate on the function of religious language. Some philosophers claimed that religious language served a different function from normal everyday speech, and that – in this context, of the realm of the infinite – the language is meaningful. Other philosophers, including the logical positivists, claimed that religious language has no meaning at all because it talks about things which cannot be proved using empirical evidence.

The logical positivists regarded religious language as meaningless because it is used to consider things beyond human experience and this leads to problems in understanding the meaning of any assertions made. The problems arise because:

- any discussion relating to God and belief cannot be based on common ground
- religious language is not **univocal** and therefore the meaning of an assertion may be unclear
- religious language is **equivocal** language because it is talking about the realm of infinite existence
- the result is different interpretations and understandings of the words used.

Activities

1 Write down how an atheist's concept of God would be different from that of a believer.

2 What problems do you think could arise when an atheist and believer try to discuss their respective concept(s) of God?

Development of the principle by Ayer

A. J. Ayer (1910–89) was a logical positivist. He believed that empirical methods have to be used to assess whether a proposition is in principle verifiable, and therefore meaningful. It is the steps taken to verify a proposition which make it meaningful. A proposition needs to be analysed to find out what is meaningful and what is not. A physicist makes propositions about the universe that at some future date may be challenged or proved untrue. Ayer considered such propositions meaningful because the physicist bases his findings on experiments. A scientific theory may not be verifiable 'in practice', but because scientists know how to verify a theory, it is verifiable 'in principle'. Ayer decided that a proposition is meaningful if it is known how to prove it true or false in either principle or practice. If it is not known how it might be proved true or false, then a proposition is meaningless. Therefore, according to the logical positivists, as religious propositions cannot be analysed using empirical methods, they are meaningless.

Strong and weak verification

Later Ayer realised that we accept some scientific and historical propositions that have not be verified with certainty. He introduced two forms of the verification principle, 'strong' and 'weak' verification, to deal with this problem.

Strong verification occurs when there is no doubt that a statement is true, as we verify it using sense experience, that is, observation. An example of a statement that would be verifiable in the strong form is, 'Mary has red hair', which could be proved true or false by seeing Mary.

Weak verification occurs where there are some observations that are relevant to proving a proposition true or false, but not enough to prove it conclusively. For example, 'Columbus discovered America' is accepted as verifiable because people affirmed the event at the time. Similarly, statements that could be affirmed in the future, such as scientific claims, are accepted as meaningful on the basis of weak verification.

Think about

'The criterion, which we use to test the genuineness of apparent propositions of fact, is the criterion of verifiability. We say that a sentence is factually significant to any given person, if, and only if, he knows how to verify the proposition which it purports to express – that is, if he knows what observations would lead him, under certain conditions, to accept the proposition as being true, or reject it as being false.'

Ayer, Language, Truth and Logic, 1936

On the basis of this statement from A. J. Ayer, why do you think he would reject propositions such as 'God is good' or 'God loves me'? Support your answer with direct quotes from Ayer.

Take it further

Read A. J. Ayer's theories in his book, *Language, Truth and Logic*, 1936 (new edition 2001).

People verified that Columbus discovered America at the time

> A proposition is … verifiable in the strong sense of the term, if, and only if, its truth could be conclusively established … But it is verifiable in the weak sense if it is possible for experience to render it probable.

A. J. Ayer, Language, Truth and Logic, *1936*

■ Take it further

Look back to Chapter 1, pp2–7. Write an explanation of how Anselm and Descartes argued that it was possible to prove the existence of God by analysing the definition of the word 'God'.

Ayer considered that empiricism cannot 'account for our knowledge of necessary truths'. He accepted analytic propositions because to reject such statements would be illogical. He accepted a priori truth in both mathematical and linguistic statements because they 'add nothing to our knowledge'. He accepted them because:

> the power of logic and mathematics to surprise us depends, like their usefulness, on the limitations of our reason. A being whose intellect was infinitely powerful would take no interest in logic and mathematics. For he would be able to see at a glance everything that his definitions implied, and accordingly could never learn anything from logical inference which he was not fully conscious of already.

A. J. Ayer, Language, Truth and Logic, *1936*

Activities

1 Write down the following statements:

- When water reaches boiling point, it turns to steam.
- Unicorns exist.
- There is life on other planets.
- A spinster is an unmarried woman.
- God exists.
- $3 + 3 = 6$.
- An occultist is an eye doctor.
- $91 \times 79 = 7{,}189$.

Decide which statements Ayer would consider meaningful and which he would reject as meaningless.

Write the reasons for your choice by each statement.

2 Write a 500–600-word essay to explain the verification principle.

The falsification principle

The falsification principle is another response to the verification principle, albeit that it maintains a similar approach to it. Many philosophers regard the falsification principle as a more serious challenge to the meaningfulness of religious language. Antony Flew developed the principle in the 1950s.

Flew applied the falsification principle to religious language, and concluded that religious statements are meaningless. Flew argued that this was because there is nothing which can count against religious statements. Religious statements can neither be proved true (verified), nor false, because religious believers do not accept any evidence to count against (falsify) their beliefs. It is important to see that for Flew there is no difference between non-falsifiability and meaningfulness.

Flew argued that Christians hold to their belief that 'God is good', whatever evidence is offered against God's goodness. To support his point, Flew uses the example of a human father desperate to save his child dying of inoperable cancer: the 'Heavenly Father' appears indifferent to the child's suffering. To account for God's indifference the believer allows nothing to count against the idea that 'God loves us as a father'.

> It often seems to people who are not religious as if there was no conceivable event or series of events the occurrence of which would be admitted by sophisticated religious people to be a sufficient reason for conceding 'there wasn't a God after all' or 'God does not really love us then'. Someone tells us that God loves us as a father loves his children. We are reassured. But then we see a child dying of inoperable cancer of the throat. His earthly father is driven frantic in his efforts to help, but his Heavenly Father reveals no obvious sign of concern. Some qualification is made – God's love is 'not merely human love' or it is 'an inscrutable love' perhaps – and we realize that such suffering is quite compatible with the truth of the assertion that 'God loves us as a father (but of course...)'. We are reassured again. But then perhaps we ask: what is this assurance of God's (appropriately qualified) love worth, what is this apparent guarantee really a guarantee against? Just what would have to happen not merely (morally and wrongly) to tempt but also (logically and rightly) to entitle us to say 'God does not love us' or even 'God does not exist'? I therefore put to the succeeding symposiasts the simple central questions, 'What would have to occur or to have occurred to constitute for you a disproof of the love of, or the existence of, God?'

Antony Flew, Theology and Falsification: Reason and Responsibility, *1968*

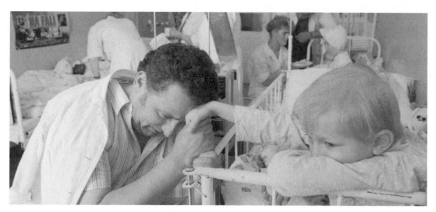

Flew argues that a human father who appears to be getting no help from God to cure his sick child qualifies his beliefs about God's love

Activity

Read the *Parable of the Gardener* opposite.

Flew said that a believer's continual refusal to accept things which count against the existence of God made any discussion about this meaningless. He said that religious statements die the 'death by a thousand qualifications'.

Write an explanation of what Flew meant by this statement. Support your answer with reference to the *Parable of the Gardener*.

Think about

- Do you agree with Flew that there is no difference between an imaginary gardener and no gardener at all?
- How does this parable illustrate the falsification principle?

Parable of the Gardener

The believer gives reasons why God remains good, and Flew stated that these constant qualifications render religious statements meaningless because they die the 'death by a thousand qualifications'. He developed a tale based on John Wisdom's *Parable of the Gardener* to prove his point that religious statements are meaningless because a religious believer will allow nothing to count against his or her beliefs.

> Let us begin with a parable. It is a parable developed from a tale told by John Wisdom in his haunting and revolutionary article Gods. Once upon a time two explorers came upon a clearing in the jungle. In the clearing were growing many flowers and many weeds. One explorer says, 'Some gardener must tend this plot.' The other disagrees, 'There is no gardener.' So they pitch their tents and set a watch. No gardener is ever seen. 'But perhaps he is an invisible gardener.' So they set up a barbed-wire fence. They electrify it. They patrol with bloodhounds. (For they remember how H. G. Well's The Invisible Man could be both smelt and touched though he could not be seen.) But no shrieks ever suggest that some intruder has received a shock. No movements of the wire ever betray an invisible climber. The bloodhounds never give cry. Yet still the Believer is not convinced. 'But there is a gardener, invisible, intangible, insensible to electric shocks, a gardener who has no scent and makes no sound, a gardener who comes secretly to look after the garden which he loves.' At last the Sceptic despairs, 'But what remains of your original assertion? Just how does what you call an invisible, intangible, eternally elusive gardener differ from an imaginary gardener or even from no gardener at all?'

Antony Flew, Theology and Falsification: Reason and Responsibility, *1968*

Differences between the verification and the falsification principles

The falsification principle differs from logical positivism in two ways:

- It depends on falsification rather than verification to decide whether or not a statement is meaningful.
- Falsification stops short of saying that we need proof that a statement is true, but demands that we know what kind of evidence we would accept to make us reject it as false. If we do not know this, then our statement would be immune to all factual knowledge, hence factually meaningless.

Remember when discussing whether it is possible to talk meaningfully about God that the falsification principle is not the only response to the verification principle.

💡 Challenges to the verification principle

Many philosophers have rejected the verification principle. The reasons for its rejection included the following:

- The principle itself is not meaningful because it cannot be verified using the verification principle.
- The 'weak' form of verification would support some religious statements. There is some sense experience that could count towards them. For example, the proposition, 'God is the creator' could

Activity

In small groups, make a list of examples of cognitive propositions and non-cognitive propositions.

Explain to the other groups your choice of propositions and the reason for your classification of them.

be supported by evidence of possible design in the world. There is historical evidence which counts towards propositions such as 'Mohamed is the Prophet of Allah' or 'Jesus rose from the dead on the first Easter Sunday'.

Some philosophers consider that a weakness of the verification principle is that it does not allow for the fact that the limitations of verifying an experience may result from limitations of the person attempting to verify it. For example, it would be difficult for a blind man to verify that the sky is blue, and therefore such a statement is meaningless to him. Yet for a sighted person, the statement that the sky is blue can be verified. It could therefore be claimed that statements about God cannot be verified by a person who does not have faith but are meaningful to those who have a shared experience of God. Flew uses the parable of the gardener to explain why a believer will not accept that religious statements are meaningless because a religious believer will allow nothing to count against his or her beliefs. However, empirical evidence is used to seek the 'gardener' whereas a religious believer would argue that God is found through faith.

This resulted in philosophers who did not accept the verification principle seeking to prove that religious language does have meaning even if it cannot be verified or falsified. Many philosophers argued that religious statements are not cognitive and it is wrong to treat them as such. Religious statements are **non-cognitive**. Religious statements do not contain facts that could be proved true or false.

The reasons for the rejection of the falsification principle include the fact that there are statements that we cannot falsify, and yet we understand the meaning behind the statement. Richard Swinburne used the example of toys in the toy cupboard to support this point. We can never prove that the toys do not come out of the toy cupboard and move around when we are not watching them. Yet although we cannot falsify the statement that the toys do not move around, we still understand the meaning behind the statement.

Do these toys come to life at night?

Religious language as a 'blik'

R. M. Hare agreed with Flew that the falsification principle could help decide the meaningfulness of cognitive statements. Although religious language cannot make factual claims, it still has meaning – not because it imparts knowledge, but because it influences the way in which people look at the world. Hare illustrated this point with the example of a university student who was convinced the dons were plotting to kill him. He would not accept any evidence that he was shown to the contrary. The student would not accept evidence that would falsify his belief, but the belief was meaningful for the student even if it was not true as it influenced the way he saw the university. The student's way of looking at the university was significant for him. Hare called this way of looking at the world a **blik**. A blik is a frame of reference in terms of which evidence is interpreted. A blik dictates how all evidence is interpreted; it cannot be verified or falsified, but it is either true (corresponding to reality) or not. The blik is not based on the evidence and therefore cannot be contradicted by the evidence. The university student was convinced that the dons were plotting to kill

Link

Look back at p21 and remind yourself of the meaning of cognitive.

Key terms

Non-cognitive: a view of religious language which argues that its function is not to inform. Non-cognitive language includes ethical or moral propositions linked to some theories of ethical language, or an expression of an emotion such as a scream.

Blik: the term used by R. M. Hare to denote a frame of reference within which everything is interpreted.

Key philosopher

R. M. Hare (1919–2002)
He was a moral philosopher important in the context of religious language for his use of the idea of a 'blik'.

Think about

Do you agree with Hare or Flew? Give reasons for your opinion.

him and so every action of the dons was interpreted within that frame of reference by the student. Religious beliefs are 'bliks' because of the impact they have on the way people look at the world and live their lives, and nothing is allowed to count against people's beliefs.

Flew condemned Hare's argument as a 'dialectical dud-cheque', meaning that Hare has not really given a reason why religious language is meaningful. According to Flew, all Hare has done is to develop the 'fraudulent substitute' of a blik.

The logical positivists reject religious language because there is no way of verifying it. Hick challenged the verification principle on the grounds that there are some propositions that cannot be verified by everyone, or to be verified it is sometimes necessary to take action. He uses the example that to verify whether or not there is a table in the next room requires one to go into the next room. Similarly, to verify a belief in life after death one first has to die. If there is life after death then the truth of 'continued conscious existence after bodily death' is proved, but as Hick points out, if there is no life after death then the fact that such a belief is false can never be falsified as the fact that it is 'false can never be a fact of which anyone has experiential knowledge'. This fact does not undermine the meaningfulness of the hypothesis of life after death, for as Hick states, 'for if its prediction is true, it will be known to be true'. Hick calls this idea **eschatological verification**. Hick is making the point that we do know how to verify propositions such as God exists, so religious statements do have meaning.

Believers do allow things to count against their beliefs

Basil Mitchell wanted to show that religious statements are meaningful even if they are not straightforwardly verifiable or falsifiable. He was trying to take a position between Flew and Hare.

Mitchell argued that Flew was wrong in supposing believers never allow anything to count against their beliefs. Mitchell claimed that Flew missed the point that believers have a prior commitment to trust in God based on faith, and for this reason do not allow evidence to undermine their faith. Believers have to look for qualifications that can explain why there is, for example, evil in the world and still accept a 'God who loves us'. Mitchell agrees that bliks exist, but he holds that a believer will allow a gradual accumulation of evidence to overturn or remove a blik.

Parable of the Freedom Fighter

To explain what he meant, Basil Mitchell provided the *Parable of the Freedom Fighter* (also known as the *Parable of the Partisan*). During the Second World War, a member of the resistance in an occupied country meets a mysterious stranger who claims to be a leader of the resistance movement, and he is to be trusted even if at times he seems to be on the side of the enemy and helping them. The resistance fighter's faith in the stranger is constantly tested. Sometimes the stranger helps members of the resistance; at other times, he is seen going into German headquarters and attending parties with German officers. Sometimes he is seen in police uniform handing over patriots to the occupying forces. However, the freedom fighter still trusts him. Sometimes the stranger is asked for help, and gives it. Sometimes the stranger is asked for help but no help is given. The resistance fighter retains his trust in the stranger and is certain that he knows best, even though others in the resistance are convinced that the stranger is not on their side. Still the resistance fighter refuses to condemn the stranger and keeps faith in him, even though he is willing to agree that at times he appears to help the enemy.

Think about

Do you agree with Hick's argument for eschatological verification? What are the reasons for your view?

Key terms

Eschatological verification: a phrase coined by Hick for the idea that some statements will be proved true after death, for example there is life after death.

Take it further

Using the internet, read Mitchell's *Parable of the Partisan*.

Activity

Explain in your own words Mitchell's argument that religious language is meaningful.

Mitchell is demonstrating that believers like the resistance fighter accept that there may be evidence against their beliefs. Mitchell states that believers should not accept beliefs that are merely a hypothesis or contain empty or meaningless statements that make no difference to their lives or experiences. However, according to Mitchell, evidence can be found which counts for and against such beliefs, but once a commitment to believe has been made, neither the partisan nor the religious believer will allow anything to count decisively against their beliefs. For Mitchell, then, religious beliefs are a matter of fact that can be proved or disproved.

Flew's response to Mitchell was that you cannot compare God to a human being. God has no limitations so why cannot God always be on our side? As Allen Stairs concluded:

> Flew sees the analogy as flawed. The stranger is a limited mortal. That makes it easy to explain why he does not always appear to be on our side. But God is not limited in any way; no excuses could be made for God's lapses. However, Mitchell could surely point out: it isn't a matter of making specific excuses. It is a matter of having faith that there is some explanation, even if we can't see what it is – of saying that we don't understand, but we trust. The question Flew would presumably ask is: don't we understand well enough?

Allen Stairs, Flew, Hare and Mitchell: A Symposium on Theology and Falsification, *1998*

Religious responses to the verification principle

A major criticism of the verification principle is that it is developed by non-believers, who in seeking to demonstrate why religious language is meaningless have failed to grasp the meaning and purpose of religious language for the believer. Often the believer is trying to convey revelations which are ineffable and therefore are aware that the meaning is not conveyed using verifiable language. Many mystics, such as St John of the Cross, believe it is possible to talk about God by not saying what He is, but by saying what He is not. This is known as the *via negativa*. The mystics resort to saying what God is not; for example, by saying that God is 'not evil' and 'not human'. By joining phrases together people learn about God. Although other philosophers agree that negative propositions take people nearer to understanding God, they do not think that they help people to understand what God is or say anything about God which is definitely true.

The *via negativa* as a principle of speaking about God was recognised by mystical writers such as St Augustine and Dionysius the Pseudo-Areopagite. The scholars argued that every positive quality attributed to God (the *via positiva*), such as that God is all-loving, all-knowing and all good, must always be balanced by the recognition that human language is inadequate when trying to describe the ineffable and indescribable attributes of God. Swinburne, with his example of the toys in the toy cupboard, supports this point that even if we cannot verify or falsify whether or not the toys move when not watched, we can still understand the meaning behind the concept.

The logical positivists themselves realised that verification by its very nature rules out many statements that we accept as meaningful, so Ayer introduced his 'strong' and 'weak' versions of the argument. Most philosophers would not consider the principle to be discredited when applied to religious language as it is generally accepted that the aim of

Think about

Do you agree with Mitchell or Flew? Give reasons for your opinion.

Key terms

Via negativa: Latin for 'negative way'. It is also known as the apophatic way and is a theology that attempts to describe God by negation, to speak of God only in terms of what may not be said about God.

AQA Examiner's tip

Explaining the problems with religious language is usually best done using examples. These can be taken from many places, including the writings of philosophers, the scriptures, hymns, poetry or your own imagination. Showing why simple statements like 'God spoke' or 'God walked' are difficult to understand allows you to explore many of the issues involved.

When you want to use the views of scholars in your assessment, think WWW – who, what and why. Knowing who they are can be impressive, but it is the least important piece of information. 'What' summarises their point of view, or perhaps quotes it. This is important, but it is not evaluation. 'Why' is the evidence and/or argument used to support that point. Focus on this and you will critically analyse, discuss and evaluate those views as required.

Link

Look back at p29. Many mystics such as St John of the Cross believe that it is possible to talk about God. How did he believe that it is possible to talk about God?

Key terms

Analogical view of religious language: the view associated with St Thomas Aquinas, that descriptive terms when applied to God mean neither the same nor something completely different than when they are applied to humanity. For example, human love may be seen to be a limited and imperfect shadow of the love God has for humanity, but there are similarities in what the word 'love' means in both contexts.

Analogy: a comparison between two things, when a similarity between two things is suggested by the use of the same word. In the phrases 'a good book' and 'a good dog', the word 'good' is not used in the same way, but there is a similarity in the way in which it is used, and so if we understand its meaning in one phrase, its use in the second will also be meaningful.

Link

Look back at Chapter 1, pp7–8. Why did Aquinas reject the ontological argument?

religious statements is not to impart knowledge about the world but to influence the way in which people look at the world, as explained by Hare's 'blik'.

In any consideration of religious language the importance of faith must not be ignored, and this is something which the verification principle has done. As Mitchell points out, a believer does not reject their beliefs even when presented with evidence against them as it is an important part of faith to retain trust that God is always working for our good. In the symposium, Theology and Falsification, Mitchell points out that once committed to his faith, a Christian is precluded from discarding his faith 'if experience tells against' it. Also, according to Mitchell the believer must allow such experiences to make a difference in their lives and not to ignore them: to do so would be 'a failure in faith as well as logic'.

The religious responses to the verification principle have demonstrated that religious language is not something that can be verified using empirical evidence because it is non-cognitive language. Therefore, a different criterion is needed for determining meaning. Some philosophers think that religious language is used as a non-literal way and through analogy, symbol and metaphor it conveys meaning about God.

Activity

Write an essay in answer to the following:

- Explain the verification principle.
- Discuss critically the strengths and weaknesses of the verification principle in relation to religious language.

Different views of religious language

Some philosophers think that it is possible to apply words that describe human qualities and characteristics to help our understanding of God. However, people need to realise that there is a difference between the way a word is used to describe human characteristics and the way in which the same word is applied to God.

Aquinas' analogical view

St Thomas Aquinas developed an **analogical view of religious language**. He argued that we only have our day-to-day language to talk about God. In the *Summa Theologica*, Aquinas stated that, 'We cannot know what God is, but rather what He is not'. We understand that a word, when applied to God, has a different meaning from its everyday use because we understand God is perfect. We are therefore using analogies.

Some philosophers have rejected the use of analogies to describe God. They argue that an **analogy** has to have some shared understanding, some basis for comparison. This is not possible when speaking about God, because God is beyond human understanding. They believe that the use of analogies within religious language is meaningless. Aquinas disagreed. He argued that there is a relationship between the world and God. God created the world, and sustains it, so there is a point of comparison. Aquinas developed two forms of analogy to talk about God:

- analogy of proportion
- analogy of attribution.

Analogy of proportion occurs when a word is employed to refer to a quality that a thing possesses in proportion to the kind of reality it possesses. For example, a dog is loyal in the way in which dogs are loyal, and humans are loyal in proportion to the loyalty of being a human. Similarly, one can understand God as all-powerful as we have the human idea of power. God is proportionally more powerful than humans, so although we cannot completely understand the idea of God's omnipotence we can have an insight into God's power because of our human experience of power.

Analogy of attribution applies when a term, originally used concerning one thing, is applied to a second thing because the one causes the other. For example, we may speak of someone having a 'sickly' look because his or her appearance is the result of sickness. Aquinas saw human wisdom as a reflection of God's wisdom. God is the source of love and life, therefore it is possible to speak of 'the Living God' or 'God loves us'.

Ramsey's models and qualifiers

Ian Ramsey developed the theory of analogy in the 20th century. Ramsey refers to 'models' and 'qualifiers'. A model is an analogy to help us express something about God. For example, if we speak of 'God as good', the model is the word 'good'. We have human understanding of 'good', and when applied to God it is a model for understanding God's goodness. Ramsey states that if we want to understand God's goodness we need to adapt the model, to qualify it, so that we realise that it is not literally what God is like. To the statement 'God is good' we need to add the qualifier that God 'is infinitely good'. This will make us think of God's goodness in greater and greater depth until eventually we have a better insight into God's goodness, and we will then respond to this insight with awe and wonder.

Activity

Write an essay in answer to the following:
- Explain the use of analogy in expressing human understanding of God.
- 'Analogy is inadequate at conveying the greatness of God'. Discuss.

💡 Religious language is metaphorical and symbolic

Another argument that supports the idea that religious language is meaningful is that it is through **metaphors** and **symbols** that we are helped towards an understanding of God. Paul Tillich (1886–1965) believed it is through metaphors and symbols that religious language communicates religious experiences. Religious language tries to interpret that experience and it is therefore:

- closer to poetry than prose
- mythical, heroic and imaginable
- evocative of the experience it seeks to describe.

Tillich believed religious language is **symbolic** because it 'opens up' new levels of reality. Tillich argued that symbols go beyond the external world to what he described as their 'internal reality'. Religious symbols 'open up levels of reality which otherwise were closed to us'. When the Bible speaks of the 'kingdom of God', the symbol of a 'kingdom' is concerned with the reality of God's power and rule. We understand a kingdom on earth, and by thinking about an earthly kingdom, we can go beyond to understand the ultimate reality of the power in the universe that is God.

Think about

- Compare Aquinas' assertion that religious language is analogical with Dionysius' use of the *via negativa* on p29. In what ways do you think the two ways of speaking about God similar, and in what ways do you think that they are different?
- Analogy fails to provide a clear, precise understanding about God. Do you think analogies allow a meaningful discussion of God and His characteristics? Give reasons for your answer, showing that you have thought about more than one point of view.

Think about

How is Ramsey's theory of analogy different from that of Aquinas and how is it similar?

Take it further

Using the internet and/or library find out more about Ian Ramsey's 'models' and 'qualifiers'.

Key terms

Metaphors: figures of speech. A word or phrase is used to denote or describe something entirely different from the object or idea with which it is usually linked in order to suggest a resemblance or analogy.

Symbols: things that stand, or are used, in place of some other thing.

Symbolic: a view of religious language which sees the words representing the reality to which they point, and in which they participate, but which they cannot describe. An analysis of religious language is found in the work of Paul Tillich.

■ **Activities**

1 Consider the word 'king'. Do you think that it would have the same symbolic impact in modern society as it would in the days of Henry VIII?

2 List other words that have lost their impact or changed their meaning in recent times.

■ **Key terms**

Archetypes: these can be seen as 'image generators'. They are distinct from the actual images they generate. Jung gave the technical name 'archetype' to the part of the psyche which creates these images.

■ **Take it further**

Read Jung's book, *Man and His Symbols* to find out more about his theory of the archetypes.

A Greek cross and a Latin cross (Greek cross on the left)

Tillich believed that a symbol 'unlocks dimensions and elements of our soul'. Religious symbols take us to 'being itself'. Tillich suggested that the power of symbols to direct ways of thinking changes through time. This is because the impact and meaning of words change, and the symbol is no longer able to direct us towards what 'concerns us ultimately' as it did in the past.

Arguments opposing religious language as symbolic

Other philosophers reject the view that religious language is symbolic. The arguments of those opposed to religious language as symbolic include:

■ Tillich who argued that symbols direct people to things beyond the symbol and in this way can lead to revelations about one's faith. However, the truth of the revelation cannot be verified or falsified using empirical evidence. Paul Edwards therefore did not believe that symbols convey any factual knowledge, and thought they were meaningless.

■ Some philosophers consider that the symbols used may not be appropriate, and yet there is no way of knowing which religious symbols are appropriate to transfer ultimate truth through things, persons and events. Tillich commented that symbols can lose their value over time and so some philosophers would argue that this means that the symbol's original meaning may be lost and the meaning conveyed has changed from what was originally intended.

■ A symbol is intended to point the way to understanding something, but some philosophers argue that it is not possible for religious symbols to successfully point the way to that which is beyond human experience. There is no way of knowing if the symbol gives the wrong insights about the ultimate reality. Symbols are about the real world. Yet Tillich does not apply symbols to an objective reality, and therefore this might lead to misunderstandings of the way in which religious symbols are understood.

Arguments supporting religious language as symbolic

The arguments of those supporting religious language as symbolic include:

■ J. R. Randall has similar ideas to Tillich and sees religious language as a human activity which makes a special contribution to human culture. Religious language has a unique function. It is able to stir strong emotion and to bind communities together through a common response to their faith.

■ Carl Gustav Jung's last book was called *Man and His Symbols*. In this book, Jung argues that several basic **archetypes** emerge as we delve into the realms of the unconscious. Jung seeks to show how particular symbols have appeared time and time again throughout history, indicating that we are never far from our basic animal psyche. He believes that the archetypes of human experience, which derive from the deepest unconscious mind, reveal themselves in the universal symbols of art and religion.

The cross as a symbol

A contemporary of Jung, Aniela Jaff, comments on the symbol of the cross used by Christians, explaining that in the early days, the equilateral or Greek cross was the usual form. But over the course of time, the centre moved upward until the cross took on the customary form of today.

She argues that this development is important because it corresponds to the inward development of Christianity. It symbolised the tendency to remove the centre of man and his faith from the earth and to elevate it into the spiritual sphere. Christians, then, were looking outside themselves for the Kingdom of Heaven, shunning earthly life, and this symbolism was reinforced by the architecture of the churches which took the eye upwards towards Heaven.

The function of symbols

Symbols serve several different functions. These functions include:

- Identifying the concept that they are conveying – for example, the use of water in Christian baptism conveys the concept of cleansing the individual of sin.

- Sharing in some way in the meaning of that concept – for example, baptism participates in the Christian belief that through the sacrifice of Jesus it is possible to remove original sin.

There are some symbols that transcend all cultures and religions, for example the symbol of light.

> ### Activities
>
> **1** Look at the painting of Christ as 'the light of the world'.
>
> Write down the message you think that Holman Hunt is trying to convey by his use of Christian symbolism.
>
> **2** Read Genesis Chapters 1–3.
>
> Write your own description of God's creation of everything and the fall of Adam and Eve.

💡 Religious language as myth

Myths are stories that use symbol, metaphor and allegory to convey a religious truth. The story itself is not true but through the story, a religious truth is conveyed. Many Christians accept that many of the stories in the Old Testament, such as the creation account in Genesis, are myths.

A distinctive use of symbolic language

Myths are another distinctive use of symbolic religious language to convey ideas beyond our own understanding. Metaphors are often used within the myth to help convey the meaning behind the story, as can be seen in the creation myths that seek to explain the origin of the universe as created by God. Myths that convey understanding of how things came about are called aetiological myths and these can be used as examples of how myths are used as a means of conveying religious 'truths'.

Aetiological myths

Aetiological myths provide foundation ideas for religious approaches. Most belief systems include creation myths to explain the origin of the universe and its components. An explanation of the origin of the universe is known as a cosmogony. Creation myths are amongst mankind's earliest attempts to explain some of the most profound questions about the nature and origin of the universe. These are questions that we are still attempting to answer today through scientific theories such as the Big Bang.

The Light of the World *by William Holman Hunt (1827-1910)*

Think about

To what extent do you think symbols are of limited use in describing God?

Key terms

Myths: stories designed to resolve philosophical or religious problems or dilemmas.

Aetiological myths: aetiology is the study of how things came about or are caused. Aetiological myths seek to explain the origin of the universe and its components.

Take it further

- Using the internet and/or library read an account of creation from another religion other than Christianity, for example Hinduism or the creation myths of ancient Egypt or Greece.
- Write this creation account in your own words.

Activity

Look at your description of the events in Genesis Chapters 1–3. List examples from Genesis 1–3 that match the themes found in creation myths.

There are some common themes to be found in creation myths. However, it should be noted that these themes or motifs are the creation of modern scholars of myths and mythology, not the people who created the myths in the first place. Any one creation myth will have several thematic features to a greater or lesser degree. This is the rule rather than the exception.

Themes in creation myths

The themes found in creation myths include:

- The existence of a chaotic formless state prior to the creation of the universe, often described as a body of water, or nothing at all (hence creation *ex nihilo*).
- A god who exists in a void performs some action which results in the universe coming into being. At some stage, usually the final stage of creation, human beings and the world as we know it come into being.

The final general aspect of creation myths, involving the creation of human beings at some stage by gods or other supernatural entities, establishes a connection between the everyday world of human beings and the supernatural world of the god or gods who created the universe. It also establishes the place of human beings in the hierarchy of life inhabiting the universe. Man is placed below gods and other supernatural beings but above animals and plants. This aspect shows us the aetiological or explanatory function of creation myths. The different cultures and religions are expressing what they regard as the truth in symbolic forms in myth.

Views of the use of religious language as myth

Many philosophers have rejected the use of myth as meaningless because of the outdated concepts that are often contained within them. For example, it could be argued that the scientific discovery of the Big Bang makes the Genesis account an anachronistic concept.

Scholars such as Rudolph Bultman argued that the language and imagery of the Gospel accounts were outdated and it is only by rejecting this mythological language that the true message of the New Testament can be found. Scholars who shared Bultman's view have gone as far as to suggest that the belief in Jesus as God incarnate is a myth. God in the human form was a myth to convey the important religious truths about God's relationship with humanity. It is because people no longer understand that these accounts are myth and not historical, literal events that has led to the decline in Christianity within a scientific age.

Other scholars have criticised this view, as they believe that to reject mythological language would be to reject much of the religious belief underlying it. In his book, *Religion and the Scientific Future*, Langdon Gilkey explored the use of myth in the modern scientific world, and argued for the continuing reality and relevance of the meaning behind the symbolic language within the myths. This is because he considered that it is through the language of myth that we understand not only how our thinking has evolved but also how our future will develop. Even if people think that religion means nothing to them, Gilkey considered that they were still influenced by the religious language of symbols and myths and that they can still help us to interpret the world in which we live.

Links

- Look back at the verification principle and the challenges to the principles on pp22–24 and 26–30.
- For a reminder of what non-cognitive means, see p27.

Think about

The verification and falsification principles seek to demonstrate why it is not possible to talk meaningfully about God, and the challenges suggest why it is possible. How successful are the arguments defending the meaningfulness of religious language?

⌐ Wittgenstein's language games

Ludwig Wittgenstein (1889–1951) originally supported the logical positivists, but he came to reject the verification principle. He decided that the meaning of words is in their use, the function they perform as agreed by the particular group or society using them. He pointed out that each activity has its own language, for example tools in a toolbox:

> Think of the tools in a tool-box: there is a hammer, pliers, a saw, a screw-driver, a ruler, a glue-pot, glue, nails and screw. The functions of words are as diverse as the functions of these objects.

Wittgenstein, Philosophical Investigations *(with a revised English translation), 1991*

The items in the toolbox are all tools, but without knowing the different functions of the tools, understanding is only superficial. Similarly the handles used to control a train look alike but have different functions, but without knowing the function of each handle then the train will not move.

> It is like looking into the cabin of a locomotive. We see handles all looking more or less alike. (Naturally, since they are all supposed to be handled.) But one is the handle of a crank which can be moved continuously (it regulates the opening of a valve); another is the handle of a switch, which has only a brake-lever, the harder one pulls on it, the harder it brakes; a fourth, the handle of a pump: it has an effect only so long as it is moved to and fro.

Wittgenstein, Philosophical Investigations *(with a revised English translation), 1991*

Wittgenstein regarded this use of language rather like a game with its own set of rules. **Language games** exist within all forms of human activity and life. People not in the game will be unable to understand the use of the language. For example, without knowing the purpose of the tools in the toolbox we cannot be a builder, and if we do not know the purpose of the handles in the train we cannot be an engine driver. If people do not understand the language, then it will seem to be meaningless. Religious belief has its own language. A non-believer will find religious language meaningless because they are not in the religious language 'game'. But an outsider cannot claim that the language used in a particular 'game' really is meaningless just because it does not make sense to them.

■ Take it further

Read Ludwig Wittgenstein's book, *Philosophical Investigations*.

■ Key terms

Language games: the name given by Wittgenstein to his claim that the uses of language are governed by rules, as games are governed by rules.

■ Activity

Try to explain the rules of cricket or some other team sport to someone else who knows nothing about the game.

What problems do you encounter?

Would 'bowling a maiden over' be meaningless to someone who does not understand cricket?

Private language

René Descartes believed he had proved his own existence because of his private thought, 'I think therefore I am'. Wittgenstein argued that individuals could not create a private language. How would individuals know that they were using words correctly? Language is a social product and therefore any thoughts are not in private but in public language, with socially agreed rules on how this is to be used and understood. Wittgenstein denied the first-person certainty which had underlined both rationalist and empiricist approaches to philosophy. This further suggests that talk about God is meaningful only in the context of the community that uses the religious language game.

Criticisms

Criticism of Wittgenstein's view of religious language have included the following:

Think about

Do you think that religious beliefs are no more than language games?

■ If people in different faiths are playing their own language game, how is it possible for there to be discussion between the different faith traditions about God's existence?

■ Religious believers are involved in other language games because they are involved in other aspects of life. This means that religious language is not totally isolated. This means that there will be common ground between religious language and other 'language games'. This common ground means that non-believers are able to understand religious language and decide whether it has meaning for them.

■ Non-believers might be able to understand religious language better than believers. This is because non-believers have an objective view of the use of religious language.

Religious language as moral discourse

R. B. Braithwaite pointed out that the error of the verification and falsification principles had been to treat religious language as cognitive language when in fact it is non-cognitive. Religious language is moral discourse because it is about the way in which people should behave towards each other. He argued, 'Theological propositions are not explanations of facts in the world of nature in the way in which established scientific hypotheses are.' Braithwaite argued that religious claims are meaningful because:

■ A religious claim is primarily a moral claim expressing an attitude. It expresses an intention to follow a specified code of behaviour.

■ It is different from a moral claim, however, in that a religious claim will refer to a story as well as an intention.

■ It is not necessary for the religious person to believe in the literal truth of the story referred to in order to resolve to live a certain way of life.

Activity

■ Read the section related to anti-realist views in Chapter 1, p17.

■ Explain the anti-realists' view of religious language.

⏷ Is it possible to talk meaningfully about God?

Supporters of the verification and falsification principle generally argue that it is not possible to talk meaningfully about God because such statements cannot be verified or falsified. Exceptions to this trend could include Hick, who suggests that religious statements can be verified eschatologically, and those who argue that certain religious statements are open to weak verification.

AQA Examiner's tip

Plan your answer before you write, and check your plan against the question when you are ready to begin writing. Have you included all of the key words in the question? If it asks you to explain religious language as analogical and symbolic, does your plan cover both? Do not miss the opportunity to write about something you actually know well simply because you did not read the question carefully enough.

Generally, however, it falls to those who reject the verification and falsification principles to defend the meaningfulness of talk about God. Many have tried to prove that religious language has a purpose because it has the function of conveying ideas. Examples of this approach include those who consider that religious language has meaning as analogy, symbol or myth.

Conclusion

Believers would agree that there is a level at which it is difficult to talk about God. The meaning of the word 'god' applies to a being beyond human understanding. Believers recognise that any discussion of God is limited, but they would argue that religious language does have meaning and/or purpose. On the other hand, some but not all non-believers might argue that God-talk is meaningless, that it is not possible to talk about God in a meaningful way because it is not possible to prove the existence of God or to verify any of the statements related to God. Many philosophers such as Wittgenstein would conclude that it is only possible to talk meaningfully about God if one has faith in God.

Further reading and weblinks

Cole, P. and Lee, J. *Religious Language*, Abacus Educational Services, 1994. The booklet considers aspects of religious language including: the verification principle, the falsification principle, religious language as symbolic and language games. It has been written specifically for A2 students of religious studies.

Davies, B. *An Introduction to the Philosophy of Religion*, Oxford University Press, 1993. In Chapter 2, Davies considers whether or not it is possible to talk meaningfully about God. Davies covers the topics of metaphor, analogy, negation and language games.

Flew, Hare and Mitchell: A Symposium on Theology and Falsification, http://brindedcow.umd.edu/236/flew.html. Allen Stairs discusses the symposium entitled 'Theology and Falsification' in which Flew issues the challenge that religious language is meaningless. Hare and Mitchell respond to Flew's challenge.

Hick, J. H. *The Fifth Dimension*, Oneworld Publications, 1999. In chapter 25, John Hick examines the use and misuse of myth with examples from Judaism and Christianity.

Jackson, R. *The God of Philosophy*, TPM (*The Philosopher's Magazine*), 2001. In Chapter 9 'Religious language', Jackson considers what is meant by religious language, whether religious language has meaning, whether we can talk about God, and religious language as a language game.

Mitchell, B. (ed.) *The Philosophy of Religion*, Oxford University Press, 1971. Chapter 1, 'Theology and falsification' is a symposium between Antony Flew, R. M. Hare and Basil Mitchell in which they discuss the meaningfulness of religious language.

Myths, Models and Paradigms: A Comparative Study in Science and Religion, www.religion-online.org/showbook.asp?title=2238. The website is broken down into chapters in which Prof. Ian Barbour compares myths, models and paradigms in science and religion. The relevant chapters are:

- Chapter 1: Introduction that covers the diverse functions of language, the role of models and the role of paradigms – to support the position of critical realism that the author defends in both science and religion.

AQA Examiner's tip

For revision, it is useful to be able to analyse one example of religious language from different perspectives. What does 'God loves me' mean? Consider the words as if they are analogical, symbolic, non-cognitive or part of a language game, for example, then apply the verification and falsification principles to them.

■ Chapter 2: Symbol and myth considers religious models in relation to other forms of religious language – particularly symbols, images, myths, metaphors, parables and analogies. The author discusses these religious forms, some of which have no parallel in science.

Philosophy of Religion: Chapter 8: Religious Language World Views and Reason, www2.sunysuffolk.edu/pecorip/scccweb/etexts/Phil_of_Religion_ text/Chapter_8_Language/Relation_of_Faith_to%20Reason.htm. The website summarises the debate between Hare, Flew and Mitchell and an outline of the parables that the three philosophers use to support their arguments related to religious language.

Now that you have completed this chapter, you should be able to:

■ explain the problem of the meaningfulness of religious language

■ explain the verification principle and the responses to the verification principle

■ explain and evaluate the different views of religious language

■ evaluate how successfully religion has responded to the challenge of the verification principle

■ evaluate how successful the various explanations of the nature of religious language are

■ assess whether it is possible to talk meaningfully about God.

3   Body, soul and personal identity

Learning objectives:

- to be able to explain the differing views about the nature and existence of soul and body and the body/soul relationship
- to understand the different notions of personal identity and personal existence, particularly post mortem
- to understand what is meant by a near-death experience
- to evaluate the evidence for survival after death
- to assess whether the notion of soul is coherent and whether there are reasonable grounds for belief in the existence of a soul.

Key terms

Immortality: this occurs when an immortal being or soul is not subject to death and cannot die.

Soul: the 'essence' of the person. The nature of the soul is much debated, but it is generally considered spiritual rather than physical and it is usually distinguished from the body and the mind. In some traditions 'soul' pre-exists the body, and in many traditions it continues after the death of the body.

Take it further

Using the internet and/or library, find out more about different understandings of the term 'soul'.

💡 What is death?

There is one thing on which all philosophers agree: that is that our earthly life in our current physical form will end. *The Stanford Dictionary* definition of death is 'the complete and permanent cessation of all vital functions in a living creature, the end of life'. All philosophers will agree with the first part of this definition, but there is disagreement over exactly what the latter part, 'the end of life', means. Many people accept death as the end of any form of existence. Others would argue that death is not the end of life, and that we continue in some form after death. There are many different ideas about the form that life after death might take. The ideas about our survival after death include:

- the continuation of our genes in our children and their descendants
- the view that we live on in our life's 'work'
- the view that we live on in the memory of others
- the **immortality** of the **soul**
- the resurrection of the body
- reincarnation or rebirth.

▪ The nature and existence of the soul

One area of debate is whether an individual survives death in the form they had in life. Is there personal existence after death? Personal existence in the context of the afterlife is the continuing existence of the individual with continuing memories. Is their personal identity continuing into the afterlife? Personal identity is what makes you 'you', such as an individual's memories, and what would establish that the person who lived after death was the same person as the one who died. If personal existence occurs in the afterlife then what form does it take?

A distinction is often drawn between the body and the soul of a human being. The body is normally seen as a physical object that lives, dies and then decomposes. The soul is generally associated with an individual's personality, decisions and free will, and is often linked to the mind; sometimes the two terms are used interchangeably. However, the identity and even existence of the soul are open to intense debate. The soul is often understood to be immaterial and spiritual rather than physical. This would enable it to survive independently after the death of the body, making it immortal in its own right. It would also raise the question of how such a soul might be considered to interact with the physical body.

An alternative approach identifies the soul more closely with the physical body, suggesting that the soul could only survive the death of the body if the body itself were resurrected. However, there is a wide range of variations upon these two approaches, meaning that they are not always easy to distinguish. Some, of course, consider that the soul does not exist at all, at least in any objective sense. According to this view, 'soul' is merely a word that some people use to describe their experience of personal identity. Some would consider even this experience to be an illusion created by the hardware of the brain.

■ Link

Look back at p39 and make sure you understand the differences between personal identity and personal existence.

■ Take it further

Using the internet and/or library find out about personal annihilation after death, and the claim that our influence lives on only in our children and in other lives that we have touched.

There are two main theories of human nature that have implications for meaningful survival after death:

■ **materialism**
■ **dualism**.

Make sure that you are clear about the distinction between materialism and dualism.

Materialism

Materialism does not accept that there is a separate part from the human body called the 'soul'. An individual is a living, physical body and nothing more. At death, the body dies and therefore the personal identity ceases to exist and there is no personal existence in the afterlife.

Materialists believe that an action is the result of a chain of events, and eventually science will be able to explain everything. Music is nothing but a set of vibrations in the air, a painting is nothing but coloured dots on a canvas, and a person is nothing but a brain attached to a body with a nervous system. What we assume to be an emotional response such as love or fear is no more than psycho-chemical reactions in our brain. Therefore, there is no distinction between body and soul.

There are two forms of materialism: the hard and soft versions.

Hard materialism

Hard materialism does not accept that an individual's characteristics are anything more than physical ones. Any idea of **consciousness** is nothing more than brain activity. There can be no separation between the body and the mind. When the body dies, so does the brain.

Soft materialism

Soft materialism accepts that not all characteristics are physical ones. Consciousness is more than just a brain process. The mind and body are related and do not act independently of each other, but the body often displays inner emotions. A physical symptom results from something that is troubling the mind. However, there is nothing we can do independent of our bodies and, therefore, our personal identity must involve our body as without this we would not exist. As with hard materialism, the belief is that when the physical body dies, then so does the mind. In the following quote, Richard Swinburne explains why another name for soft materialism is 'property dualism':

> The second view in the history of thought about the mind/body problem is the view which I shall call 'soft materialism'. It is often called 'property dualism'. Soft materialism agrees with hard materialism that the only substances are material objects, but it claims that some of these (that is, persons) have mental properties which are distinct from physical properties. Brain-events certainly often cause mental events and vice versa. Neurones firing in certain patterns cause me to have a red after-image. And – in the other direction – trying to move my arm causes the brain-events which cause my arm to move. These are causal relations between distinct events – just as the ignition of gunpowder is a distinct event from the explosion which it causes.

Richard Swinburne, The Possibility of Life after Death, *2004*

A summary of the materialist argument for not accepting survival after death is:

- Life depends on a functioning brain, nervous system and physical body.
- Death involves the destruction of the brain, the nervous system and physical body.
- Therefore, a person's life ends at death as life without a physical form cannot be supported.

The body/soul relationship

The body/soul relationship is much debated. For example, they are sometimes seen as two separate substances linked during life, but in other traditions the soul needs a body in order to function.

Dualism is the opposite view to materialism. Dualism accepts that there are two distinct parts to the human: a body and mind (soul) that are distinct from each other. A dualist approach to mind and body argues that the mind determines our personality and the body is an outer shell for the real self. The body is contingent and therefore is destined for decay, but the mind, associated with the higher realities, such as truth, goodness and justice, is immortal. If an individual spends life in contemplation of these higher realities, then his/her soul can enter eternity after the death of the physical body. The belief that the soul continues after death is known as the immortality of the soul. Note that not all dualists regard the continued existence of the soul to be dependent on contemplation of such higher realities as truth, goodness and justice.

Materialism and the body/soul relationship

The major disagreement between materialists and dualists is the relationship between the body and the soul during life and after death.

Most hard materialists believe that there is no such thing as a soul and that humans are no more than their physical bodies. All materialists believe that when the physical body dies the individual ceases to exist. They do not believe in an immortal soul that continues after death.

All materialists consider that there is no scientific evidence for the existence of a soul, and that as such an area is inaccessible to scientific activity then it would never be possible to prove whether a soul exists. Materialists do not accept that it is possible to locate the soul in any part of the body. The body is matter alone so there cannot be a soul.

Materialists use 'soul' synonymously with 'mind'. Many materialists would be happy to talk about a mind (although hard materialists would probably see this as merely an illusion thrown up by the 'hardware' of the brain). Soft materialists would be somewhat vague about the soul, but would argue that it is not separate from the body and could not continue to exist after the death of the body. Generally for materialists the 'soul' is used in the sense of the immaterial 'I' that is distinct from the body.

'The ghost in the machine'

Gilbert Ryle (1900–76) was a materialist. In his work *The Concept of the Mind* (1949), Ryle argued that the idea of soul – which he described as 'the ghost in the machine' – was a 'category mistake'. He argued that to speak of a soul was a mistake in the use of language. This results in people speaking of the mind and the body as different phenomena, as if the soul was something identifiably extra within a person. He used the example of a foreigner watching a cricket game and asking, 'But where's

Think about
- Do you consider yourself more than 'a body with a nervous system'?
- Is an emotion more than a chemical reaction in your brain?
- How do you know this?

Link
Look back at Chapter 1, p14 to remind yourself of the meaning of contingent.

AQA Examiner's tip
Remember that you can draw material from more than one topic when you answer a question. Any reference to the word 'soul', for example, comes up against many of the problems linked to religious language, so a question asking for an explanation of a statement like 'my soul will live on' is inviting you to include in your answer a brief consideration of whether the words mean anything at all.

Link
How do you think the logical positivists would view the idea of the existence of a soul? Remind yourself of their philosophy by rereading Chapter 2, pp22–24.

Think about

- Ryle does not accept that it is right to talk of 'mental processes' as a separate function, independent of the body.

- Why does he describe this idea of a separate mind as 'the ghost in the machine'?

- Look back at Wittgenstein's language games in Chapter 2, pp35–36.

- Why do you think Wittgenstein might argue that Ryle is mistaken in describing references to the soul as 'a conjunction to the body' as a misuse of language, 'a category error'?

Take it further

Read Gilbert Ryle's argument against the existence of a soul in *The Concept of Mind*.

the team spirit?' The foreigner expected 'the team spirit' to be something identifiably extra to the players, umpires, scorers and equipment. Ryle argued that any talk of a soul was talk about the way in which a person acted and integrated with others and the world. It was not something separate and distinct. To describe someone as clever, irritable or happy did not require the existence of a separate, invisible thing called a mind or soul. Such terms simply refer to the way someone behaves.

> When two terms belong to the same category, it is proper to construct conjunctive propositions embodying them. Thus a purchaser may say that he bought a left-hand glove and a right-hand glove, but not that he had bought a left-hand glove, a right-hand glove and a pair of gloves … Now the dogma of the ghost in the Machine does just this. It maintains that there exist both bodies and minds; that there occur physical processes and mental processes; that there are mechanical causes of corporeal movements. I shall argue that these and other analogous conjunctions are absurd; but, it must be noticed, the argument will not show that either of the illegitimately conjoined propositions is absurd in itself. I am not for example, denying that there occur mental processes. Doing long division is a mental process and so is making a joke. But I am saying that the phrase 'there occur mental processes' does not mean the same sort of thing as 'there occur physical processes' and therefore, that it makes no sense to conjoin or disjoin the two.

Gilbert Ryle, The Concept of Mind, *1949*

Activity

Write an explanation of why Gilbert Ryle considered reference to a soul as a 'category mistake'.

Scientific support for materialism

Many philosophers and scientists argue that modern science has shown there are links between the brain and the body and therefore that the mind cannot survive on its own. These materialists reject any idea of survival of a soul once the physical body is dead. One such scientist is Richard Dawkins.

Dawkins has written several books to support Darwinian evolution. Dawkins is an atheist and rejects any concept of an immortal soul. Writing in *River Out of Eden* (1995), Dawkins puts forward a case for biological materialism:

> There is no spirit-driven life force, no throbbing, heaving, pullulating, protoplasmic, mystic jelly. Life is just bytes and bytes and bytes of digital information.

Richard Dawkins, River out of Eden, *1995*

Key philosopher

Richard Dawkins (1941–)
He is an evolutionary biologist and atheist who argues against a supernatural creator and life after death.

Take it further

Read Richard Dawkins' book, *River out of Eden*, and make notes on his views about survival of personal identity after death.

Humans are 'robot vehicles'

For Dawkins there is no pre-existent soul that is by nature divine. Dawkins argues that scientific beliefs are supported by scientific evidence and are reliable. By contrast, religious beliefs, such as the concept of soul, depend on myth and faith, and for this there is no empirical evidence. Dawkins claims that the belief in a soul results from the human inability to accept that evil and suffering have no purpose. Each individual is the product of evolution with no immortal soul that survives death. The purpose of life is DNA survival, and the only way in which a human survives in any form is through their DNA locked up in living bodies – humans are no more than DNA carriers that will ensure the survival of the species.

> The true utility function of life, that which is being maximized in the natural world, is DNA survival. But DNA is not floating free; it is locked up in living bodies, and it has to make the most of the levers of power at its disposal. Genetic sequences that find themselves in cheetah bodies maximize their survival by causing those bodies to kill gazelles. Sequences that find themselves in gazelle bodies increase their chance of survival by promoting opposite ends. But the same utility function – the survival of DNA – explains the 'purpose' of both the cheetah and the gazelle.

Richard Dawkins, article in Scientific American, *November 1995*

If we are no more than the 'robot vehicles blindly programmed to preserve the selfish molecules known as genes' described by Dawkins, then how is our awareness of our individuality to be explained? Dawkins explains this sense of individuality by our genes working together as a unit. Humans perceive themselves as a whole and this is necessary if the genes are to survive. Awareness that an action results in bad consequences stops repetition, whereas when an action results in good consequences it can be repeated. Through evolution, consciousness has developed in humans so that they are able to choose the behaviour that is more likely to lead to survival of their genes for the purposes of reproduction.

In his book *The Selfish Gene* (1976), Dawkins argues that in nature the battle for survival is between the genes that encode the very nature and operation of each entry. Dawkins has developed a CD-ROM which creates electronic life forms and demonstrates how they evolve generation by generation, at the same time showing how their fitness to survive and multiply responds to changes in their computer-generated universe.

Dawkins believes in human dignity

Although Dawkins rejects the existence of an immortal soul in favour of an evolutionary process, he still believes in human dignity passed on to future generations through an individual's genetic code. He argues that the mere fact that humans have evolved to a stage where they are trying to discover the meaning of life is far more marvellous than any creation myth. Dawkins does not think that humans should worry about the meaning of their lives and their place in the hostile universe, as they are the universe.

Dawkins argues that human thinking has gone awry because people have tried to find meanings to life, for example through religious doctrine that teaches the rewards of paradise. If people rejected notions of an afterlife and a God and learnt to reason as scientists, then they would become better humans. This is because science can answer questions about the origin of life and provide evidence to support the answer, but religion can only depend on faith.

Link

Do you think you now know what is meant by personal identity? If you are still unsure look back to p39 to remind yourself of the meaning of the terms 'personal identity' and 'personal existence'.

Think about

Dawkins rejects any belief in an afterlife. Others believe that the body decays but an individual's thoughts survive. If an individual's thoughts are the only things that survive after death, does it mean personal identity has ceased to exist? Am 'I' no longer in existence?

■ Key terms

Meme: analogous to the gene, and invented by Richard Dawkins to describe how Darwinian principles might be extended to explain the spread of ideas and cultural phenomena. This is the theory of memetics. Memes include tunes, catchphrases, quotes and teachings that lodge in the brain where the brain imitates them. Dawkins has argued that it is through a meme that an individual can become immortal.

Substances: things that are able to exist independently of something else. A substance is able to exist on its own.

■ Think about

If it is not for the rewards of Heaven, why does Dawkins believe that humans should perform good actions?

■ Activity

Write an explanation of why materialism presents a problem for a believer in life after death.

■ Key philosopher

Plato (c.428–c.347 bce)
He was a pupil of Socrates and a major influence on the development of Western philosophy.

■ Take it further

Using the library and/or internet, find out about Plato's beliefs about life after death.

The meaning of meme

Dawkins concludes that the evolution of consciousness has removed the need for gene replication. There is a new replicator, human culture, that Dawkins calls a **meme**. It is through a contribution to human culture that the meme results in cultural survival within the individual. Some philosophers would consider this development of individual consciousness as what others would call the soul.

Dualism and body/soul relationship

Plato and the Forms

Plato was a dualist. He believed that the soul and the body were two separate **substances** that interact. Writing in *The Republic*, Plato stated that the soul belonged to a level of reality higher than the body. He thought that the soul is a substance and is immortal. This view derived from his theory of ideas, which he called 'the Forms'. For everything in existence, Plato accepted that there was the perfect idea (form). For example, for every man there is an ideal man, for every dog there is an ideal dog, and so on. Every individual thing participates in these universal ideas. The idea is prior to the individual instance of it, and is thus more real. Ideas are not physical things, so they must belong to a spiritual realm of reality, which is more real than the material realm.

For Plato, the real identity of the person lies within the soul, which pre-exists its present embodied form. The soul is that which can grasp the realm of ideas. It is not matter, which is gross and unthinking. The physical world is the world in which the body exists and through which we receive sense impressions. The soul is immaterial and capable of knowing eternal truths beyond the world. The soul wants to travel into the realm of heavenly ideas and to understand them; the body wants to be involved in worldly matters to do with the senses. The soul is trying to steer the mind to the spiritual realm.

For Plato, all knowledge is recollection of things remembered from previous lives which are forgotten when we are reborn. According to Plato we do not learn things in life; we only have recollection of the knowledge gained when we were in the realm of the Forms before our immortal souls became imprisoned in our physical bodies. All knowledge is the uncovering of the universal truths: the Forms. We can only recollect in this life what we knew before this life, as the soul does not forget what it learnt.

As Plato saw it, hope of survival comes naturally to the philosopher, whose whole life is one of preparation for death. What happens when we die is that the human soul separates from the human body, and it is concern for the soul rather than the body that characterises a philosophical life. In fact, Plato argued that since knowledge of the most important matters in life is clearest to the soul alone, attachment to a mortal body often serves only as a distraction from what counts as the body leads us to lesser concerns such as eating and reproduction. Plato taught that the aim of the soul is to break free of the chains of matter and flee to the realms of ideas, where it will be able to spend eternity in contemplation of the true, the beautiful and the good. The thinking being can survive without the physical body. The body does not survive death, but the soul – the real essence of the person – continues, and for Plato this is our personal identity that makes the 'I' of the person.

Aristotle and the soul

Aristotle was the pupil of Plato but he did not believe in an afterlife or in the immortality of the soul (**psyche**). In *De Anima*, Aristotle describes the mind (**nous**) as the part of the soul which reasons, it is 'the part of the soul by which it knows and understands'. He considered the *soul* to be the part of the body – which gave it life. It is what turns the physical form into a living organism of its particular type. For example, a dog has a doggy soul, and a human has a human soul. Aristotle had no problem understanding how the soul and body work together; soul and body are inseparable. The soul develops the person's skills, character or temper, but it cannot survive death. Body and soul are a unity, and when the body dies the soul ceases to exist. This would appear to be materialistic, but Aristotle did believe that the body and soul were separate but neither would survive after death. Human beings have a soul or self that is capable of an intellectual life. Only humans can reflect on feelings and sensations, and grasp 'universals' (for example, the concept of goodness as opposed to an individual good thing). This way we come to understand eternal truths.

For the ancient Greeks, the psyche, our sensations and emotion, were on the 'body' side of the mind/body dualism. If a person is hungry then the body feels hunger pangs, but the soul would dwell on the universal concept of hunger not individual hunger pangs. Aristotle refers to emotions as 'affectations of the soul'. The example he discusses is anger:

> It seems indeed to be the case that with most affectations, the soul undergoes or produces none of them without the body – being angry, for instance.

Aristotle, De Anima

Aristotle believed that the body and soul, in this instance, were inseparable in as much as they relied on and supported each other. Indeed, he went on to suggest that it is often impossible to focus purely on the material (body) or the rationale (mind) in different contexts. Aristotle did not agree with Plato that the two could be separated.

💡 Cartesian dualism

René Descartes was a dualist. In Descartes' conception, the rational mind (soul) is an entity distinct from the body and makes contact with the body at the pineal gland. He included in the 'mind' all of the feelings and sensations that he could describe but which he could not locate physically. He accepted that everything that is non-physical becomes part of the mind. Descartes argued that while we can doubt material existence, we cannot doubt our own existence – 'I think therefore I am'. Even if we are dreaming, or under the control of a demon, we must still exist to have our own thoughts. Therefore the physical and non-physical are distinct substances with distinct properties. The physical self takes up space but the mind is of a different substance that does not need to take up space. The mental reality is not empirical and therefore not in the world of space. The mind is not located in the body and is not the same as the brain. Descartes' dualism of mind and body rested on certain ideas. These included the following:

- The mind is a 'non-corporeal' substance which is distinct from material or bodily substance.
- The mind and body are different things.

Key terms

Psyche: for the ancient Greeks this was another word for the soul.

Nous: for the ancient Greeks this was the thinking part of the mind.

Key philosopher

Aristotle (384–322 BCE)
He was a pupil of Plato but had different ideas about life after death. His philosophical ideas were to influence the development of Christian thinking.

Activity

Write a 500–600-word essay explaining the similarities and differences between the understanding of Plato and Aristotle concerning body and soul.

Take it further

- Read Aristotle's primary investigation of the mind in *De Anima* iii, 4 and 5.
- Read René Descartes' arguments for dualism in his work *Meditations on First Philosophy*.

Link

Look back to Chapter 1, p5 to find out about René Descartes.

- Every substance has a property or a special character. So, for instance, the property of the mind-substance is consciousness and the property of bodily – or material – substance is length, breadth or depth. The mind is a substance 'whose whole essence is to think', and so it takes up no space. The body is material, whose essence is to take up space.

- Unlike the mind, the body is extended. It has a material form which can be described in forms of extensional features such as its size, shape, position or movement.

For Descartes, 'ideas' were in the mind, not out there in the world waiting to be grasped. **Cartesian** dualism may be summarised as follows:

- The mind is the place in which only the person experiencing them knows all feelings, sensations and thoughts.

- The body performs all physical activities. These are observable to all.

- The mind and body interact with each other as the mind can cause events to occur in the body and the body can cause events to occur in the mind.

- The mind and body are separate.

Descartes concluded that as our identity comes from our ability to think and reason, then it was conceivable that we could survive without our bodies and remain the same person. He did not accept that we need our bodies to live an intellectually aware and active life. Therefore, Descartes believed the mind could survive the death of the body. For him, the mind gives personal identity, which thinks and makes us who we are. We can drastically change our bodies and our physical appearance without changing our personalities, and even if a person underwent a radical physical transformation, we would still be able to recognise them by reference to their character and memories.

The Christian view of the person

Most Christians cannot accept Cartesian dualism because the Bible presents a **psychosomatic** view of the person that differs from Cartesian dualism. According to the Bible, God has created humans as a unity of mind (psyche), body (soma) and soul. The soul is not a separate nature from the body but it is the 'spark' that gives life to the physical body.

Aquinas' beliefs about the soul

St Thomas Aquinas agreed with Aristotle, that it was the soul which animated the body and gave it life. He called the soul the *anima*: that which 'animates' the body.

> Now that the soul is what makes our body live; so the soul is the primary source of all these activities that differentiate levels of life: growth, sensation, movement, understanding.

Aquinas, Summa Theologica, 1267–73

According to Aquinas, the soul operates independently of the body. Aquinas believed that only things that are divisible into parts decay. The soul is not divisible, therefore based on Aquinas' argument it is able to survive death. However, through the link with a particular human body, each soul becomes individual. So even when a body dies, the soul that departs retains the individual identity of the body to which it was attached.

Key terms

Cartesian: the term used for the influence of ideas and concepts developed by René Descartes.

Psychosomatic: the constant and inseparable interaction of the mind (psyche) and the body (soma).

Activities

1. List examples of ways in which the mind can affect the body and ways in which the body can affect the mind.

2. Write an explanation of Cartesian dualism.

Think about

Why, as a Christian, do you think, it was important to Aquinas that each soul should have an individual identity?

Link

Do you think you now know what is meant by personal identity and consciousness? If you are still unsure look back to pp39 and 40 to remind yourself of the meaning of these terms.

💡 ✅ Personal identity and death

What form would survival after death take?

If there is survival after death then the question arises as to the form this survival takes. Some philosophers argue that there is no subjective (personal) survival or survival of a soul after death and therefore the only way in which an individual survives is in the genes that are passed on to their descendants or by some contribution to society that is remembered. For example, we remember Shakespeare because of his plays, and we remember soldiers from the First and Second World Wars because their names are on war memorials.

Other philosophers and most religious believers do accept that there is some form of survival after death. However, this raises questions about what form that survival might take and whether the individual is still recognisable and the same person as the one who lived and died. There are three suggestions as to how personal identity might be retained:

- The person retains the same body after death (**resurrection** of the body).
- The person's body dies but the person retains the same soul after death (immortality of the soul).
- The person's body and soul die but something of their consciousness is retained.

Resurrection of the body

Not all materialists accept that death is the end: instead, some believe that there is life after death. The physical body and the 'soul' (mind) cannot be separated so there is only one way this could happen: continuation of the whole body after death. This survival would have to involve the resurrection of the body.

A dead body is known to decay in the grave or to become ashes after cremation. This raises the question of how the body could be resurrected. This presents a problem for those materialists who accept life after death. If, for a materialist, survival must include both body and soul, then life after death would have to be in a form similar to life in this world. It would have to be possible to recognise the resurrected person as the same individual that he or she was before death. Any other form would mean that the personal identity (the 'I') of the individual had not survived death. This problem led to the development of the **replica theory** or recreation theory.

💡 John Hick's replica theory

Hick is a materialist in that he believes that the body and soul are one, and at death, both the body and soul die. Hick argues that, given certain circumstances, it would be possible that the dead could exist after death as themselves, if an exact replica of them were to appear. This replica, identified as being the same person who had died, is, according to Hick, the same person. God is all-powerful; it is no problem for God to create a replica body of the dead person. This replica will be complete with all the individual's memories and characteristics, and is therefore the same person. Hick believes that although death destroys us, God recreates us in another place:

> as a resurrection replica in a different world altogether, a resurrection world inhabited only by resurrected persons. This world occupies its own space distinct from that with which we are

Think about

Brian Davies asks if an individual given a lethal dose of poison would be consoled in accepting the poison if they were told a replica of themselves would appear the instant they died.

Activities

1. Read St Paul's teaching on resurrection in Thessalonians 4.

2. Write an explanation of the teaching of Hick and St Paul about the resurrection of the body.

Take it further

Using the library and/or the internet, find out more about resurrection in Judaism and Islam.

Think about

- Would a replica body still have my personal identity?

- Is a replica body identical to the person who has died, or is it a clone of 'me', and therefore not really me?

now familiar. That is to say, an object in the resurrection world is not situated at any distance or in any direction from the objects in our present world, although each object in either world is spatially related to every other object in the same world.

John Hick, Philosophy of Religion, 1990

Hick considered that he was demonstrating that the resurrection of the body is logically possible. It is only a small step to say that a person can therefore experience *bodily resurrection* in a place where resurrected bodies dwell.

Resurrection in Christianity

Hick's view is compatible with a Christian understanding of the resurrection of the body. St Paul wrote in his letter to the Corinthians:

Someone will ask, 'How can the dead be raised to life? What kind of body will they have?' You fool! When you sow a seed in the ground it does not sprout to life unless it dies. And what you sow is a bare seed, perhaps a grain of wheat or some other grain, not the full-bodied plant that will later grow up. God provides that seed with the body he wishes; he gives each seed its own proper body. And the flesh of living beings is not all the same kind of flesh, animals another, birds, another, and fish another. And there are heavenly bodies and earthly bodies; the beauty that belongs to heavenly bodies is different from the beauty that belongs to earthly bodies. The sun has its own beauty, the moon another beauty; and even among stars there are different kinds of beauty. This is how it will be when the dead are raised to life. When the body is buried, it is mortal; when raised, it will be immortal. When buried, it is ugly and weak; when raised, it will be beautiful and strong. When buried it is a physical body; when raised it will be a spiritual body. There is, of course, a physical body, so there has to be a spiritual body.

1 Corinthians 15: 35–44, Good News Bible, 1976

St Paul taught that after death, the body will be raised, but it will be transformed and will become a spiritual body, as unlike its earthly form as the seed is from the plant into which it grows. This is one way to explain how an individual keeps the personal identity that he or she had in life but is able to achieve eternal life in a bodily form.

The problem of personal identity and a replica body

Other philosophers have criticised Hick's replica theory as they argue a replica is not the original and therefore THE individual has not survived his or her death. In the same way, an art expert would not be prepared to pay millions of pounds for a replica painting of the *Mona Lisa* however much it looked like the original.

Even if others can recognise me in my 'new' body, and I have the same memories as before I died, many philosophers do not accept that a replica body is still the same 'I' that died. It is a question of which of the following statements is accepted as correct:

- First I existed in this world, then I died, and then I existed again in the next world.

- First I existed in this world, then I died, and then God created someone else who is exactly similar to me.

Hick's response

Hick tried to solve the problem with a series of thought experiments, to prove that the 'I' that existed in this world is the same 'I' as resurrected in the next. He imagined a man called John Smith, who lived in the US. One day, his friends watched as Smith suddenly vanished without trace. At the same moment as he disappeared, a replica Smith appeared in India. According to Hick, this Smith:

> is exactly similar in both physical and mental characteristics to the person who disappeared in America. There is continuity of memory, complete similarity of bodily features including fingerprints, emotions and mental dispositions. Further, the 'John Smith' replica thinks of himself as being the John Smith who disappeared in the United States. After all possible tests have been made, and have proved positive, the factors leading his friends to accept 'John Smith' as John Smith would surely prevail and would cause them to overlook even his mysterious transference from one continent to another, rather than treat 'John Smith' with all of John Smith's memories and other characteristics, as someone other than John Smith.

John Hick, Philosophy of Religion, *1990*

Would you pay a million pounds for a replica of Leonardo da Vinci's original painting Mona Lisa?

Hick continued by supposing that John Smith died. God recreated John Smith in the next world and this recreated 'John Smith' was the same person. A further criticism of Hick is that he is relying on the existence of God to create the replica and as the existence of God is not proven then neither is the replica theory.

The immortality of the soul

A dualist approach argues that the mind (soul) determines our personality and that the body is only an outer shell to house the real self (the mind/soul). The body is contingent and therefore is destined for decay, but the mind, associated with the higher realities, such as truth, goodness and justice, is immortal. If an individual spends life in contemplation of these higher realities, then his soul can enter eternity after the death of the physical body. This belief that the soul continues after death is called the immortality of the soul.

Descartes agreed that when an individual dies, their soul can continue to exist with God, as the same individual that existed in a physical form on earth.

> Our soul is of a nature entirely independent of the body, and consequently … it is not bound to die with it. And since we cannot see any other causes which destroy the soul, we are naturally led to conclude that it is immortal.

Descartes, Discourse on the Method, *1637*

Activity

Write a 500–600-word essay assessing the strengths and weaknesses of Hick's replica theory.

Think about

Before you read the next section, do you agree with Hick that the John Smith who materialised in India is the same John Smith who disappeared in the US? What are the reasons for your view?

Link

Look back to p39 to remind yourself of a definition of the immortality of the soul.

Think about

How does the Christian psychosomatic view of the soul lead to a different view of life after death from that of Cartesian dualism?

Although most Christians accept a belief in an immortal soul that survives after death, they do not agree on whether or not it is a physical or spiritual resurrection. Many Christians believe that the physical body decays and it is an immortal soul that continues after death. God breathing life at the moment of creation is regarded as evidence by many Christians of the existence of a soul that gives human beings their individuality.

> The Lord God formed the man from the dust of the ground and breathed
> Into his nostrils the breath of life, and the man became a living being.

Genesis 2:7

Christians do not agree whether the resurrected form is identifiable with the person supposed to have survived death. If there were no physical body then there would have to be some other means by which identification takes place. It may be some aspect of the individual's nature that is recognised by others, or it could be God who ensures that individuals are recognised in the next world.

Personal identity and an immortal soul

Many philosophers are concerned that the separation of body and mind (soul) raises several questions. These challenges to dualism include the following:

■ Is our identity only the result of memories and actions in the mind? If we get a new body then does this have no influence on how we behave or how others react to us? Bernard Williams rejected this conclusion. Williams argued that memories are not a good guide to identity. Memories and personality can be fabricated so personal identity cannot be proved through mental activity alone. He believed that identity comes from physical characteristics as well. Personal identity depends on the way in which we recognise each other, and without our bodies, we cannot be fully identified.

■ What about the causal effects between mind and body? We know that there are things that we do to the body which affect the mind. For example, the use of alcohol or drugs changes personality. Similarly if people are depressed physical symptoms can be produced.

■ Modern science has shown links between mind and brain so how can the mind survive on its own? Surgeons can split the brain and create 'two minds'. The mind appears to be causally dependent upon the 'brain'.

■ If minds are non-physical objects, how can the mind cause anything to happen in the physical world? For example, if my mind is not linked to my body, then how does my thought that I will run for the bus cause the physical action of running to happen?

🔘 *Psychological continuity or connectedness*

'Sameness of consciousness'

The philosopher John Locke (1632–1704) thought that personal identity consisted neither in sameness of body nor in sameness of soul but, rather, in what he called 'sameness of consciousness'. For Locke it is consciousness that creates personal identity. He claimed that consciousness is enclosed in a spiritual substance. There is therefore a difference between a human and that human's personal identity. What he meant was that an individual should remember enough of their past

Think about

If an individual's thoughts are the only things that survive after death, does it mean personal identity has ceased to exist? Am 'I' no longer in existence?

Think about

Do you think that you are a soul that is temporarily lodged in a physical body?

Take it further

Using the internet and/or library find out more about John Locke's beliefs about personal identity.

states of consciousness, and it is this awareness of self in different places and times that is the personal identity. This means that an individual can have different bodies and yet still have continuity.

Locke used the example of the soul of a prince transferred from the prince's body into the body of a cobbler whose soul has departed. The prince still has princely thoughts and his personal identity as a prince, even though his body is different. Therefore, according to Locke, he is still the prince even though 'he would be the same cobbler to everyone besides himself'.

Locke holds that consciousness can be transferred from one soul to another, and that personal identity goes with consciousness. Locke considers that consciousness can be transferred from one substance to another and thus while the soul is changed, consciousness remains the same and thus personal identity is preserved through the change. This would support **reincarnation** or rebirth as a means by which personal identity continues after death.

Scientific theories of consciousness

The recent work of Stuart Hameroff and Roger Penrose supports the survival of consciousness at the moment of death. Penrose argues there is an essentially non-**algorithmic** element to human thought and human consciousness because humans are capable of independent thought. Penrose claims that it is **quantum** effects in the brain that are the source of our feelings of self-awareness, our consciousness and our capacity for leaps of inspiration. Hameroff and Penrose conclude that consciousness is not the product of direct brain activity but arises from tube-like structures made of proteins that exist in all the cells of the body. Because of their structure and shape it is the microtubules that are at the site of the quantum processes in the brain.

The theory is that these microtubules can change and develop in nanoseconds and support brain activity at all levels including information processing, transmission and learning. The significance of their research for life after death is the suggestion that when the body is under threat of death then the microtubules are able to leave the body so that the individual's consciousness survives. If death does not occur then the microtubules return to the brain and the individual may have a memory of being in another 'place'. As yet there is no suggestion as to how long these microtubules can survive outside of the brain or whether or not they could continue into another world or body.

> **Key terms**
>
> **Reincarnation:** the transfer of a soul or spirit from one body at death to a new one at birth.
>
> **Algorithmic:** an algorithm is a clearly defined set of steps for carrying out some procedure. Computers function using algorithms and can only do what they are programmed to do.
>
> **Quantum:** quantum theory relates to the physical laws applying to the microscopic level. Quantum theory suggests that at this level, matter behaves randomly rather than deterministically and in accordance with algorithms.

It is there at the most basic level of the universe that Hameroff and Penrose believe that consciousness occurs. Concerning the well established field of relativity, Einstein said that everything, matter, energy, space and time, and the very fabric of the universe works on the tiniest scales, and that it is at this level that consciousness may exist, within the processes of the microtubules, which could explain how NDEs [near-death experiences] occur. The microtubule coherence pumping activity stops, it leaks out, it is not lost or destroyed, [it] leaks out into the universe at large. It spreads out but hangs together due to another strange phenomenon, of quantum coherence. By this mechanism it is possible for consciousness to exist at least temporarily outside the body, floating above the body, floating above the body observing resuscitation. Hameroff's study can give us a glimpse of what life after death may be like, into a world where we don't have the technology or capability for scientific understanding.

■ **Take it further**

■ Using the internet find out more about the work of Hameroff and Penrose on consciousness, and the objections to their theory.

■ Write an account of their work and its significance for survival after death.

■ **Link**

Do you think you now know what is meant by reincarnation? If you are still unsure look back to p51 to remind yourself of the meaning of the term.

Key terms

Post mortem: after death.

AQA Examiner's tip

Be careful not to confuse similar terms. Resurrection, reincarnation, rebirth and replica theory all appear in this chapter and it is important that you know what each one refers to. If you get them muddled it could cost you a lot of marks. Answers should also make good use of such specialist vocabulary.

Criticisms

However, many scientists reject this theory of consciousness. Their arguments include:

■ The microtubules exist throughout the whole body and not just the brain.

■ Drugs exist that damage the microtubules but appear to leave consciousness unharmed.

■ The neuroscientist Sir John Eccles argues from his work on brain cell connections that the unity of consciousness is provided by the mind and not by the neural machinery of the brain.

The possibility of disembodied existence

Price's dream world

H. H. Price examines whether or not it is coherent to accept the existence of a disembodied soul, that is, a mind or soul without a body. Price compares the world in which the disembodied soul lives to a dream world. As a dream takes place within its own space and not in reality so the soul would have its own space that is not within this physical world. Also, just as dreams take place in the mind so the soul in the afterlife would be mind dependent. Price is making the point that the experiences in the afterlife are similar to dreams where we have experiences and are able to perform actions with our dream bodies. The life lived in this 'dream' world would be shaped by the individual's deepest desires and memories. We would communicate with other souls through telepathy, and the communication with another mind would include an appropriate image of the other person so that recognition occurs.

Criticisms

Hick points out that if in this disembodied **post-mortem** existence our desires are to be fulfilled then tension is going to result from conflicting desires. For example, if I wish to have dinner in Heaven this evening with Elvis but Elvis has a desire to perform in a concert this evening, which dream world do we inhabit this evening: whose dream takes priority?

Many people consider that the most important part of life after death would be the opportunity to make moral progress and to have real relationships. The only way in which this could occur if Price's dream world is to be kept is if God gave everyone the same 'dream' in the next life.

Reincarnation

Although Judaism, Christianity, Islam, Hinduism and Buddhism believe in life after death, they teach radically different things about what it is. In Judaism, Christianity and Islam the belief in an afterlife is based on a linear view of time. That means these religions believe each person will live on this earth once and after that go to be judged by God, 'Just as man is destined to die once, and after that to face judgement' (Hebrews 9:27), whereas in Hinduism and Buddhism the belief is that time is cyclical. This means they believe people do not live and die just once but are able to be reborn a number of times before reaching their final end state. The belief that after death the soul (or a person) is reborn in this world to live a new life is called *reincarnation* in Hinduism and *rebirth* in Buddhism.

Reincarnation and rebirth involve an individual's soul inhabiting a new body, which may be totally different from that of the previous life. In each reincarnation, the 'soul' lives a different life in a different body. At death the soul moves (migrates) from the dying body into a new body and this is sometimes called the 'transmigration of souls'. The aim is that through each lifetime the soul will improve itself, until it achieves perfection. When achieved, the soul will not be reborn and will enter a state of bliss.

If the survival of personal identity after death depends on the survival of bodily continuity then reincarnation has to be rejected as a means by which an individual survives death because in each life the soul enters a new body. However, if it is accepted that the person who dies is the person who is judged post reincarnation or rebirth, then there is survival of personal identity after death.

Some philosophers consider that survival of personal identity after death depends on the continuation of personal memories or traits. As within Hinduism and Buddhism memories of previous lives are either non-existent or deeply buried in the subconscious, then these philosophers would reject the notion of personal survival after death if there is reincarnation or rebirth. However, other philosophers would disagree and suggest that this is an oversimplification of the beliefs about life after death within these faiths and although the individual may be a different person within each successive incarnation there is the same continuing psychic structure carried from life to life.

Reincarnation and Hinduism

Hindus believe that the *atman* or soul is eternal. Each soul is at one with the whole of creation. In Hinduism, emphasis is placed on individual development through the cycle of life, death and reincarnation (*samsara*) to achieve release from the cycle of birth and death and to be reunited with Brahman (the Godhead). This reunification is called *moksha*. By living in the right way according to the faith (their *dharma* or duty), an individual achieves good **karma**; but by disregarding the teachings of the faith, then bad karma will influence the quality of the next life. Karma is the acceptance that there is a relationship between what a person does and what happens to them. The consequences of an action may not be experienced in this life but may influence the next. Events that happen to people in the present life may be the result of actions in past lives. Good or bad actions build up good or bad karma, and will influence events in the next life and whether an individual is reborn to a higher or lower situation.

Before *moksha* is achieved the reincarnated soul passes through many births and deaths.

> Just as a man discards worn out clothes and puts on new clothes, the soul discards worn out bodies and wears new ones.

Bhagavad Gita, 2:22

Hindus believe that a reincarnated soul carries no personal attributes from each life but the immortal essence (*jiva*) of the *atman* continues into each life. As Hick states:

> the jiva registers and thus 'embodies' the moral, aesthetic, intellectual and spiritual dispositions that have been built up in the course of living a human life, or rather a succession of such lives.

John Hick, The Fifth Dimension, 2004

Think about

How does the view that survival of personal identity after death depends on memories differ from Locke's view (on pp50–51) that personal identity consists of sameness of consciousness that supports reincarnation as a means by which personal identity is maintained after death?

Key terms

Karma: the moral law of cause and effect. Each action has a consequence and the consequences may be felt in future lives.

■ **Take it further**

Using the internet and/or library find out more about Hindu beliefs about reincarnation.

■ **Key terms**

Rebirth: this is a continuing process of change from one life to the next and arguably from one moment to the next.

■ **Take it further**

Using the internet and/or library find out more about Buddhist beliefs about rebirth.

■ **Think about**

What point about personal identity and rebirth do you think the monk was making with his analogy of a chariot?

Between each reincarnation the *jiva* learns new lessons to take into the next life. Hindus believe that each person must have experienced many lives, as the human is too complicated for this development to have taken place in one lifetime. Many Hindus point to the theory of evolution as scientific support for the belief in reincarnation.

Rebirth

In some religions, **rebirth** rather than reincarnation is the preferred term, because reincarnation is regarded as meaning that a fixed entity is reborn. Those religions who use the term 'rebirth' do consider that there is continuity between each life but that they are not identical.

Rebirth and Buddhism

Buddhists deny that there are souls. The Buddha taught that it is not an individual soul but an ever-changing individual character which moves from rebirth to rebirth. This could be considered as the consciousness of the person surviving from life to life. This belief can be illustrated by the idea of a flame being transferred from one candle to another. In the same way, the consciousness transferred between one life and the next is not identical but neither is it completely distinct. There is therefore continuity, and Buddhists accept that there is an interconnection between each life lived by a person. Each life interconnects with each previous life through the law of karma and, as in Hinduism, the quality of the next life is influenced by the good or bad karma of the previous ones. The 'I' is not the person living his or her current life but the union of all lives lived. There are causal connections between different lives, and it is through this connection that each life is part of the same person and it is this individual who is judged after death. The Buddhist monk Nagasena explained this connection using the analogy of a chariot.

'Explain to me what a chariot is. Is the pole the chariot?'

'No, reverend Sir!'

'Is then the axle the chariot?'

'No, reverend Sir!'

'Is it then the wheels, or the framework, or the flagstaff, or the yoke, or the reins, or the goad-stick?'

'No, reverend Sir'

'Then is it the combination of pole, axle, wheels, framework, flagstaff, yoke, reins and goad which is the chariot?'

'No, reverend Sir!'

'Then is this "chariot" outside the combination of pole, axle, wheels, framework, flagstaff, yoke, reins and goad?'

'No, reverend Sir'

'Then ask as I may, I can discover no chariot at all. Just a mere sound is this "chariot". But what is the real chariot?'

'Where all constituent parts are present, The word "a chariot" is applied. So likewise where the skandhas are, the term "a being" commonly is used.'

E. Conze, Buddhist Scriptures, *1983*

Personal identity and reincarnation and rebirth

If reincarnation and rebirth are correct then all those who seek it are working towards their own annihilation, as the ultimate goal is to lose personal identity and become one with the Godhead. Many westerners find this a difficult concept to accept.

Materialists would argue that, even if this process were to be possible, reincarnated or reborn individuals would enter new bodies, have different brains and lead different lives, so could not have the same personal identity as they did in previous lives. Each individual would be born to a new life with a new identity.

Many philosophers and scientists claim that personal identity depends on self-consciousness, which is an awareness of self and the individuality of self. However, with each new life there would have to be a new awareness of self, meaning that a new identity had been formed. Others argue that, as there are so many definitions of consciousness, it cannot be used to reject the idea of personal identity continuing through many lives. William Savage has compared reincarnation to going to sleep at night.

> We go to sleep at night and enter a different state of consciousness, but we awake in the morning as a continuation of the same consciousness as that of the previous day. In much the same way, reincarnation is a continuation of consciousness after death.

William A. Savage, 'Reincarnation: A Continuation of Consciousness', Sunrise magazine, *June/July 1998*

There is a belief that there is evidence to support reincarnation and rebirth because people have memories of past lives. Such memories would also support Savage's view that there is a continuation of consciousness from one life to the next. For example:

- There are people, especially children, who claim to have memories of former lives. Historical records have confirmed some of these descriptions of past lives.
- Others appear to have regressed to earlier lives under hypnosis, and some of these memories have been investigated and found to be accurate accounts of people and places from the past.

Not all investigators accept these 'memories' as evidence of reincarnation and put forward other reasons for an individual possessing such knowledge. These include:

- The individual might be remembering information gained in childhood and mistakenly interpreting this as a past life.
- There could be a cultural gene which passes down information about the lives of our ancestors.
- Some memories may be the result of psychological problems that manifest themselves as memories of earlier lives, when in fact they are suppressed events from this life.

The question arises therefore as to whether these memories of a former life can be classed as 'proof' of earlier lives or the existence of a soul.

Think about

Look back at Locke's example of the prince and the cobbler on p51. Would Locke's argument challenge the view that a reincarnated or reborn individual is a different person?

Activities

1. Find out what the term 'déjà vu' means.

2. Do you think the experience of déjà vu is a memory from a past life or an electrical discharge in the brain?

Link

Look back to p52 to be sure that you understand the term 'post mortem'.

Link

If you are not sure what the word 'coherent' means, look at the definition on p60.

Is the notion of a personal post-mortem existence coherent?

The question raised here is whether or not statements such as 'I will survive the death of my body' or 'I will have a bodiless existence after death' or 'I will exist in a new replica body after death' are coherent.

However, there is other evidence to support personal post-mortem existence and therefore to make such notions coherent. These include:

- sightings of dead people
- spiritualism
- near-death experiences.

Are ghosts evidence of survival beyond death?

Some people regard sightings of dead people as evidence of survival after death. However, there is controversy as to whether ghosts would be evidence of:

- resurrection of the body, as they seem to have a recognisable physical form similar to how they would have looked in life
- immortality of the soul, as although recognisable as individuals, ghosts do not appear to have material bodies because they can pass through walls
- the existence of a consciousness beyond death that supports reincarnation or rebirth.

Think about

Would a belief in ghosts support the resurrection of the body, immortality of the soul or the existence of consciousness? Give reasons for your opinion.

Criticisms

Some argue that ghosts are genuine manifestations of dead people rather than hallucinations because often more than one person sees them. There have been sightings at the same place, by different people, at different times. However, if a ghost is not a sighting of a dead person, then other explanations for the phenomena include the following:

- Hoaxes or elaborate tricks to make people think they have seen a ghost.
- The 'stone tape' theory suggests that just as magnetic tape is able to record events and play them back, so, in certain conditions, stones will record dramatic events and 'play them back' when the same conditions are present.
- Ghosts could be mistaken identity (such as a trick of the light) or the power of suggestion that leads to the mistaken belief that a ghost has been sighted.
- Dr Deepak Chopra pointed out that bodies are comprised of energy. Ghosts may appear solid but the truth is that they are just an impulse of energy. When an individual dies, the energy field may retain his or her image and be perceived as a ghost. He considers the 'ghost' to be the imprint of an individual's consciousness, manifesting itself through the remaining energy and not evidence for any form of personal survival after death.

Key terms

Spiritualism: the belief that it is possible to communicate with departed spirits. The communication between those who have 'passed over' and those in this world takes place through a medium. A medium is an individual believed to have the ability to receive messages from those in the spirit world and pass them on to the living.

Think about

If spiritualism were proved to be true, in what form would individuals have survived their death?

Activity

Write an essay in response to the statement, 'Any evidence put forward to support life after death is no more than wishful thinking'.

Is spiritualism evidence of survival beyond death?

Many regard **spiritualism** as evidence of life after death because it involves communication between those who have died and are in the spirit world, and the living. Many mediums have passed on messages from departed spirits that contain accurate information, which was previously unknown to the medium. These messages give comfort to the bereaved as they suggest that their loved one is still 'alive' in another dimension, and that at some future date they will be able to join them.

Criticisms

Investigations of some mediums have proved that they are frauds. Others appear to be genuine, and to demonstrate that something extraordinary is happening when they pass on messages. It could either be communication from departed spirits, or some form of telepathic access to the minds of those who are still living. There is evidence to support both points of view.

💡 Near-death experiences as evidence of survival beyond death

Advances in modern technology have resulted in more people who have been declared clinically 'dead' subsequently being resuscitated. Dr Raymond Moody realised that the descriptions by these people of what happened to them while they were 'dead', were so similar that it must be more than coincidence. His research into the phenomenon of **near-death experiences** demonstrated that although no two near-death experiences are the same, they share common features. An individual who has a near-death experience may not experience all of the features. The most common feature is the feeling of being drawn down a tunnel towards a light.

In 1983, Professor Bruce Greyson devised a measurement scale to differentiate between near-death and other experiences. The experience is graded according to the features experienced and the intensity of the experience. To be classified as a near-death experience there must be a minimum score of seven out of a maximum of 32. According to the Greyson Scale the features of a near-death experience are that the person experiences:

- an altered state of time
- accelerated thought processes
- a life review
- a sense of sudden understanding
- feelings of peace
- feelings of joy
- feelings of cosmic oneness
- feeling/seeing that they are surrounded by light
- vivid sensations
- extrasensory perception
- a vision of some future event
- a sense of being out of the physical body
- a sense of an 'other-worldly' environment
- a sense of a mystical entity
- a sense of deceased or religious figures
- a sense of a border or point of no return.

Remember that the term 'near-death experience' is the term used to describe the out-of-body experience of people who have been declared clinically dead and have subsequently been resuscitated. The term is not referring to people who have escaped from a situation in which they could have died, for example people who survive a plane crash or road accident.

Generally, it is agreed that near-death experiences are genuine in that something happened to the individual during the time that he or she was declared clinically dead. However, there is disagreement as to whether or not a genuine out-of-body experience occurred or whether the experience is evidence for life after death.

Key terms

Near-death experiences: the term used to describe the out-of-body experience of people who have been declared clinically dead and have subsequently been resuscitated.

Ascent of the Blessed *by Hieronymus Bosch (c.1490)*

Activity

The main challenge to near-death experiences is that they are *near* death. Those who reject the experience as evidence of life after death argue that the individual did not die and the experience had other causes such as oxygen starvation. Make a list of reasons that might be given to account for what happened to the 'dead' person by those who argue that it is not a genuine out-of-body experience.

Activity

Using the internet and/or library find out more about Dr Melvin Morse's research into NDEs.

Evidence to support near-death experiences

Those who support near-death experiences as an out-of-body experience and evidence for life after death use the following evidence to support their belief:

■ Those who have the experience have a clear recollection of what occurred during the experience that is different to what occurs to people in dreams or under the influence of anaesthetics. Dr Peter Fenwick's research demonstrated that of those he investigated, who had a near-death experience, only 14 per cent had received any form of drug.

■ The near-death experience is life changing. After the experience, individuals have a belief that the most important thing in life is love of others. People become more interested in spiritual rather than material things and more concerned with the welfare of others.

> One thing is clear, that NDEs have extreme effects on the people who have them. Most people who have these experiences are profoundly changed. They become less materialistic, competitive, less involved in personal power, prestige and fame, much more concerned about relationships with others, and with the spiritual side of their lives. People change their careers. And while NDEs have changed lives, they have given some people experiences, that they never would have dreamt of having.

The Ground of Faith Journal, October 2003

Dr P. M. H. Atwater, who has researched the experience, writes on her website:

> No matter what the nature of the experience, it alters some lives. Alcoholics find themselves unable to imbibe. Hardened criminals opt for a life of helping others. Atheists embrace the existence of a deity, while dogmatic members of a particular religion report feeling welcome in any church or temple or mosque.

Atwater, www.cinemind.com/atwater/

■ Those who have a pleasant near-death experience no longer fear death and, for those whose experience is negative, there is a certainty that they must change their way of life if they are to avoid punishment in the afterlife. For example, having spent his life in a wide variety of crimes, after an unpleasant near-death experience in which he saw 'souls' suffering, a man called Ronald Regan converted to Christianity and became a preacher working with convicts.

■ Children declared clinically dead are able to give accounts of near-death experiences without understanding what they are describing. The experiences of children under seven are significant, as they will not have heard of the phenomenon and will not have preconceived ideas of what happens after death. Yet children report near-death experiences similar to those described by adults. The paediatrician Dr Melvin Morse's research of near-death experiences in children has led him to accept that the experiences are 'genuine'. He has concluded from his research that memory may be stored outside the brain and the right temporal lobe acts as a transmitter and receiver between the individual and God.

People witness events while clinically dead that they later describe. This includes blind people describing people and objects which they would not normally be able to see. When researched these descriptions prove to be accurate accounts of events. The most notable example is the experiences of Pam Reynolds whose heart and brain function were stopped in order to operate on an aneurysm in her brain. The exact moment at which her brain activity ceased is known, and therefore the evidence that she provides of what happened while she was clinically dead cannot have been acquired by hearing or seeing what occurred during the operation.

Near-death experiences occur in all parts of the world and affect people regardless of race, creed, sex or age. There is evidence of the experiences throughout history. The common features of all these experiences and the life-changing effect of the experiences suggest that something more than starvation of oxygen to the brain has occurred, and make it unlikely to be a psychological or hallucinatory experience.

Opposition to near-death experiences as evidence of post-mortem survival

Those who oppose the near-death experience as an out-of-body experience and evidence for life after death put forward the following scientific arguments for the causation of near-death experiences.

The exact point at which the individual 'died' or is resuscitated is not known, and as the last sense lost is hearing, patients may have heard discussion of their condition. Upon resuscitation, the brain constructs the near-death experience from stored memories of what they heard and what they know of hospital procedure.

The experience is described as a near-death experience because the individual was not dead and therefore the experience has nothing to contribute to the knowledge of what happens after death.

Near-death experiences are the result of **hypoxia**. The dying brain creates feelings of euphoria and feelings of being in the presence of a supernatural being. Dr Persinger is a **cognitive neuroscience** researcher, who argues that near-death experiences are no more than the brain responding to external stimuli. Persinger claims that by stimulating the temporal lobes he can artificially induce feelings similar to near-death experiences. Dr Persinger has developed a helmet which produces weak magnetic fields across the hemispheres of the brain, specifically the temporal lobe. The superior parietal lobe, the centre that processes information about space, time and the orientation of the body in space, is suppressed, and is almost totally quiet while the pre-frontal cortex, which contains the temporal lobe, that controls attention, is highly stimulated. There is suppression of any sense of time, space or being in the world along with the activity in the superior parietal lobe. In addition, not feeling 'in the world' leads to an 'other-worldly' experience similar to the near-death experience.

American jet fighter pilots have had similar experiences to near-death experiences when spun at high levels of acceleration ('+Gz') in a human centrifuge. As the pilot loses consciousness due to lack of blood flow to the brain there are often feelings of euphoria, and floating down a dark tunnel towards a light.

Dr Susan Blackmore has developed the 'dying brain' hypothesis. Normally the majority of our vision comes from our central vision and very little from our peripheral vision. She argues that as the brain dies, the lack of oxygen to the brain activates cells at the back of the brain that are involved with central vision and this creates the

Take it further

Using the internet find out what happened to Pam Reynolds and why her experience is supportive of the near-death experience as evidence of life after death.

Think about

Why do you think that the fact that people of different cultures and ages experience NDEs makes it unlikely that the experience is a hallucination?

Think about

Do you think that what happened to Pam Reynolds undermines the argument that patients' claims to an awareness of what happened while they were clinically dead are no more than a reconstruction of what they saw and heard before they 'died' or as they were resuscitated?

Key terms

Hypoxia: a deficiency of oxygen reaching the tissues of the brain.

Cognitive neuroscience: the study of the nervous system, and cognitive neuroscience is the branch of neuroscience that studies the biological foundations of mental phenomena such as religious experiences.

Think about

Although the pilots have experiences similar to NDEs, there is no evidence that the experiences are life changing for them. Does this suggest that they have not had a near-death experience?

Link

Look back at the work of Hameroff and Penrose relating to consciousness on p51.

Think about

- Does Hameroff and Penrose's theory relating to consciousness support NDEs? Does their theory support the idea of some form of life after death?

- What are the reasons for your opinion?

impression of an intense bright light. However, as fewer of the cells associated with peripheral vision are activated the vision narrows and the sense of going down a tunnel is created. The brain then begins to create images to replace the outer images lost by the loss of vision.

- Freudians regard near-death experiences as hallucinatory wishful thinking to overcome the fear of death. Hallucinations often appear very real to those who experience them.

Activity

To help you assess whether or not you think that NDEs are evidence of life after death, divide a piece of paper into two columns.

Label one column 'In favour of NDEs as evidence for life after death' and the other 'Against NDEs as evidence for life after death'.

Using the information in this section and your own research complete the columns.

Evaluate each column and decide whether NDEs make it reasonable to believe in the existence of life after death.

Is the notion of the soul coherent?

This is the first question that needs answering according to all the evidence available from both religion and science. As we have seen in this chapter, there are divergent views as to whether the soul and consciousness are the same thing and whether the soul is separate to the physical body. Which view we accept depends largely on our prior beliefs and this may also affect the extent to which the concept of the soul is considered **coherent**. For example, Christians accept the existence of the immortal soul as the core of the individual person, partaking of his or her choices and deeds, and which survives death. However, although they agree that there is an immortal soul that survives the death of the physical body, Christians disagree on the manner of its survival. Buddhists and Hindus agree that the soul in some way continues into many lives but disagree as to whether this occurs through reincarnation or rebirth.

Key terms

Coherent: used here to mean that the notion of the soul is logically consistent and easy to understand.

The notion of soul is not coherent

One argument that the notion of soul is incoherent comes from the view that if souls were immaterial and unattached to bodies, there would be no individual souls with their own personal identities because there would be no boundaries between them that would enable us to separate them.

Another problem with coherence of the soul is the very idea that a non-physical soul can have existence (and even 'substance') and be able to influence or be influenced by the physical body.

Link

Look back to Chapter 2, pp22–24 and remind yourself of the verification principle of the logical positivists.

The logical positivists rejected any reference to 'soul' as meaningless and therefore incoherent. This is because under the verification principle we can only know the meaning of a statement if we know the conditions under which the statement is true or false. As it is not possible to know how to prove the existence of a soul within the human body, then the logical positivists regard any notion of a soul as meaningless and illogical.

The notion of soul is coherent

John Hick's theory of 'eschatological verification' would support the notion of soul as coherent. Hick argued that when we die we will know the truth of what happens after death. Therefore, the truth as to whether a soul exists will be proved true or false (verified).

Whether the immortality of the soul, resurrection of the body, reincarnation or rebirth are accepted, there is one common feature and that is that in some way an individual continues in some form after death.

Link

Look back to Chapter 2, p28 and remind yourself of Hick's theory of eschatological verification.

Are there reasonable grounds for belief in the existence of the soul?

The first question that occurs to most philosophers is whether there is any good reason to believe in life after death. Is there sufficient reliable evidence to support a belief in the existence of the soul after death?

The problem is that it is not possible to prove, beyond any shadow of doubt, the existence of soul; and much less, the form the soul takes and whether or not it survives death. Each individual has to weigh up the evidence and decide whether or not there are reasonable grounds for belief in the existence of the soul and with it reasonable grounds for the belief in the afterlife. Research into what is consciousness and NDEs may provide some evidence but as John Hick asks:

> Do these accounts describe the first phase of another life, or perhaps a transitional stage before the connection between mind and body is finally broken; or do they describe only the last flickers of dream activity before the brain finally loses oxygen? It is hoped that further research may find a way to settle this question.

John Hick, Philosophy of Religion, 1990

Further reading and weblinks

Atwater, P. M. H. www.cinemind.com/atwater/. Dr Atwater's website provides a comprehensive survey of the near-death phenomena.

Comparative Religion – Reincarnation in world religions, www.comparativereligion.com/reincarnation.html. This article presents the reincarnation theory in the major eastern religions and some of its possible inconsistencies.

Davies, B. *An Introduction to the Philosophy of Religion*, Oxford University Press, 1993. In Chapter 11, Davies examines philosophical questions raised by the possibility of life after death.

Hick, J. H. *Death and Eternal Life*, Harper & Row, 1980. The book provides a broad survey of the major issues relating to body, soul and personal identity.

Hick, J. H. *Philosophy of Religion*, Prentice Hall International, 1990. Chapter 10 on human destiny: immortality and resurrection examines issues relating to immortality of the soul, the recreation of the psychophysical person, parapsychology and resuscitation cases.

Jackson, R. The God of Philosophy, *TPM* (*The Philosopher's Magazine*), 2001. Chapter 11 considers the mind-body problem and evidence for life after death.

Moody, R. A. *Life After Life: The Investigation of a Phenomenon – Survival of Bodily Death*, HarperOne (part of Harper Collins), 2001. Raymond Moody investigates more than one hundred case studies of people who experienced 'clinical death' and were subsequently revived. First published in 1975, it was this book that led to the study of near-death experiences.

The Case for Life After Death, www.leaderu.com/truth/1truth28.html. Professor Peter Kreeft considers the reasons for accepting that there is life after death.

The Possibility of Life after Death, http://people.pwf.cam.ac.uk/dhm11/Swinburne.html. The web page has Richard Swinburne's contribution to 'An Afterlife', a symposium that was part of 'Death: a Live Issue', a Humanist Philosophers' Group conference on death and dying held at King's College London on 19 October 2002. It presents Swinburne's arguments for the possibility of life after death.

Webber, J. *Philosophy of Religion 6: Life After Death*, Abacus Educational Services, 1996. The booklet considers aspects of life after death including: the significance of death, beliefs about life after death and evidence for life after death. The booklet has been written specifically for A2 students of Religious Studies.

Now that you have completed this chapter, you should be able to:

- explain the differing views about the nature and existence of soul and body
- explain the differing views about the body/soul relationship
- explain what is meant by a near-death experience
- evaluate the notion of personal post-mortem existence
- evaluate the evidence for survival after death
- assess whether the notion of soul is coherent and whether there are reasonable grounds for belief in the existence of soul.

The problem of evil

Learning objectives:

- to understand the concept of evil (natural and moral)

- to understand the logical and evidential problem of evil

- to understand religious responses to the problem of evil

- to evaluate the success of the theodicies and process thought as a response to the problem of evil

- to evaluate whether free will is a satisfactory explanation for the existence of evil in a world created by God

- to evaluate whether natural or moral evil poses the greater challenge to faith in God.

Key terms

Evil: that which is contrary to God's will; a cause of suffering. This definition is only of relevance to religious people.

Moral evil: intentional human action (commission) or inaction (omission) that results in suffering, for example murder, or, arguably, failure to have children vaccinated.

Natural evil: causes of suffering within the natural world including disaster, disease, decay and death.

Link

Look back at Chapter 1, p1 to remind yourself what is meant by the God of classical theism.

💡 The concept of evil

One of the main arguments used by non-believers against the existence of God is based on the presence of evil and suffering in the world. The term **'evil'** is often used to describe something that is morally wrong. Hence, crimes like mass murder are often called evil. However, philosophers make a distinction between **moral evil** and **natural evil**.

Evil is often divided into natural and moral evil although the distinction may be blurred in cases where intentional human actions (for example, knowingly building on a fault line) exacerbate the effects of natural disasters (earthquakes etc.).

Natural evil: 2004 Indian Ocean earthquake and tsunami

The consequence of evil is suffering. Suffering often involves mental anguish and depression as well as physical pain. These effects can be very long lasting; many participants in the two world wars never recovered from their ordeals. In addition to the pain that it causes, suffering is often unjust. It strikes indiscriminately, so that its victims are often those who have done nothing wrong, including tiny babies.

Activities

1 Look at the picture of the 2004 Indian Ocean earthquake and tsunami above. It is estimated that more than 275,000 people were killed on 26 December 2004 when an undersea earthquake, with its epicentre off the west coast of Sumatra in Indonesia, triggered a series of tsunamis that devastated the coasts of most landmasses bordering the Indian Ocean.

- Is this event a form of moral or natural evil?

- Why is this event considered to be evil?

2 Explain the two types of evil in the world and support your definitions with three examples for each type.

- Which of these two types of evil do you think it would be harder for a religious believer to accept? What are the reasons for your choice?

Take it further

Using the internet and/or library find out more about the view propounded by J. L. Mackie and make your own notes about his view.

Key terms

The problem of evil: the challenge that the existence of evil poses for faith in God. Two forms of the problem are generally recognised: the logical problem of evil based on the inconsistent triad; and the evidential problem of evil based on the existence of pointless suffering which, it is argued, makes it probable that God does not exist.

The logical problem of evil: the view propounded by J. L. Mackie, and also found in the work of David Hume among many others, that the three statements: 'God is all-powerful', 'God is all-loving', and 'there is evil in the world', are logically inconsistent and cannot be true. Since one of the three (evil exists) appears to be true, at least one of the other two must, logically, be false.

The problem of evil

The devastating effects of natural and moral evil are unpleasant for everyone who is affected by them. However, for religious people evil poses an additional challenge to their faith which is known as **the problem of evil**. This is the problem of how an all-powerful and all-loving God can allow His creation to suffer without coming to its rescue and putting an end to its torment.

It can be seen that the problem of evil is a challenge specifically for believers in the God of classical theism. Other religious outlooks, which accept the existence of a variety of gods of assorted character and authority, do not have the same problem since the existence of evil can be attributed to the tensions between the different gods. However, followers of the God of classical theism acknowledge the existence of one God only, who is the all-powerful and all-loving Creator of the universe. The problem of evil challenges this belief and comes in two forms:

- **The logical problem of evil** argues that evil makes the existence of God impossible.
- The evidential problem of evil argues that evil makes the existence of God improbable.

The logical problem of evil

The logical problem of evil argues that the existence of evil is incompatible with the existence of God. As a result, it is logically inconsistent to accept that both exist together. This can be summarised as the following dilemma:

- Since God alone created the universe out of nothing, He has total responsibility for everything in it. If He is omnipotent, then He can do anything that is logically possible. This means that He could have created a world free from actual evil and suffering, and free from the possibility of ever going wrong. It also means that, should He have allowed them to come about, He could end all evil and suffering.

- Since God is omniscient, He has complete knowledge of everything in the universe, including evil and suffering. He also knows how to stop it.

- However, if God is all-loving, He would wish to end all evil and suffering. In the words of J. L. Mackie, 'A wholly good being eliminates evil as far as it can' (*The Miracle of Theism: Arguments for and against the Existence of God*, 1982). Any *loving* being, as we understand the term, would wish to stop the multiple horrors heaped upon the millions of innocent people over the years. No *all*-loving God would allow His creation to suffer physical and mental torment for no reason and to no avail. Since God is omnipotent, He could immediately carry out his desire to step in and stop the suffering.

- Upon examining the qualities of omnipotence, omnibenevolence and evil, David Hume argued that only two of the three can exist alongside each other. Therefore, *either* God is not omnipotent, *or* God is not all-loving (omnibenevolent) or evil does not exist.

- While the existence of evil has been questioned by some, Hume considered that its effects are felt too widely, and its presence attested too vividly for it to be dismissible. Therefore, accepting that evil exists, he concluded that God must either be impotent or malicious.

Either way, this entails the death of the God of classical theism. Hume therefore concluded that God cannot exist.

The problem of evil is often given in the form of an **inconsistent triad**. For example, Epicurus gave the following three propositions:

- Evil and suffering exist in the world
- God is all-powerful
- God is all-loving

Epicurus argued that these propositions were inconsistent and thus that there could be no all-powerful, all-loving God.

 Activity

Imagine you have toothache and are trying to describe it to a friend who has no idea what it feels like.

How could you convince your friend that you are in pain?

Would it be unreasonable for your friend to doubt the truth of your claim?

Can God and evil both exist?

Hume's position is supported by an argument found in Aquinas' *Summa Theologica*, which suggests that God's existence in the face of evil is *logically* impossible:

> It seems that God does not exist: because if one of two contraries be infinite, the other would be altogether destroyed. But the name of God means that He is infinite goodness. If, therefore, God existed, there would be no evil discoverable; but there is evil in the world. Therefore God does not exist.

Aquinas, Summa Theologica, *1267–73*

Since, for Aquinas, the concept of infinite goodness is an essential part of God's nature, any proof against God's goodness being infinite will constitute proof that God does not exist. The existence of even the tiniest quantity of evil precludes the possibility of infinite goodness. As witnesses to the evil in our world, we are thus witnesses to proof against the existence of God.

However, Aquinas differed from Hume in that whereas Hume, as an atheist, accepted this conclusion, Aquinas went on to reject it. Despite drawing attention to the apparently insurmountable contradiction between God and evil, Aquinas remained one of the most famous Christian thinkers of all time.

This is possible because Aquinas' logical argument only works if we accept its two premises:

- The concept of infinite goodness is part of the definition of God.
- In talking about God's *goodness*, we are referring to the same thing as human goodness, and assuming that what we call evil is incompatible with the goodness of God.

 Key terms

Inconsistent triad: this consists of three propositions of which at most two can be true. For example:

- John loves Mary.
- If John loves Mary, he would have asked her to marry him.
- John has not asked Mary to marry him.

One of the three propositions of an inconsistent triad has to be given up or modified as all three statements cannot be true. Maybe John does not love Mary, or maybe he would not ask Mary to marry him if he did love her, or maybe he has already proposed.

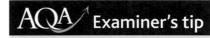 **Examiner's tip**

Remember that it is the combination of God's qualities that is the dilemma in the logical problem of evil. You would need to explain carefully why it is argued that since evil exists in the world God cannot be both all-loving and all-powerful. It is not enough to simply state that it is impossible, or to use quotations to show that someone else thinks it is impossible.

Activity

Write an explanation of the logical problem of evil.

 Examiner's tip

In your explanation of the logical problem of evil make sure that you include references to the views of J. L. Mackie, David Hume and Aquinas.

The evidential problem of evil

The logical problem of evil argues that the existence of the God as defined by classical theism is logically incompatible with what is known about evil and the suffering it causes. The **evidential problem of evil** argues that what is known about evil and suffering is *evidence* (rather than *proof*) against the existence of God, which is therefore improbable.

William Rowe's evidential problem of evil

William Rowe develops one form of the evidential problem of evil and argues his case for atheism in *The Problem of Evil and Some Varieties of Atheism* (1979). Rowe bases his argument around the form of evil that he describes as the 'intense human and animal suffering' that 'occurs on a daily basis' and 'is in great plenitude in our world'. Rowe accepts that if this evil and suffering resulted in 'some greater good' that could only be achieved by its presence, then such suffering might be justified even though it would still be considered evil even if the final outcome was good. However, Rowe argues that this type of suffering is *not* all required for a greater good, and that it is therefore evidence against God's existence:

1 There exist instances of intense suffering which an omnipotent, omniscient being could have prevented without thereby losing some greater good or permitting some evil equally bad or worse.

2 An omniscient, wholly good being would prevent the occurrence of any intense suffering it could, unless it could not do so without thereby losing some greater good or permitting some evil equally bad or worse.

3 Therefore there does not exist an omnipotent, omniscient, wholly good being.

William Rowe, The Problem of Evil and Some Varieties of Atheism, *1979*

Rowe considers it a valid argument that a God who is able to do anything and who is wholly good would not permit evil that is avoidable, pointless and in no way fulfils His purpose for the world. The evidence that such evil exists is therefore taken as evidence that God cannot exist.

To support his argument Rowe provides several examples of pointless human and animal suffering. These include the following.

An example of human suffering

The girl's mother was living with her boyfriend, another man who was unemployed, her two children, and her nine-month old infant fathered by the boyfriend. On New Year's Eve all three adults were drinking at a bar near the woman's home. The boyfriend had been taking drugs and drinking heavily. He was asked to leave the bar at 8:00pm. After several reappearances he finally stayed away for good at about 9:30pm. The woman and the unemployed man remained at the bar until 2:00am at which time the woman went home and the man went to a party at a neighbour's home. Perhaps out of jealousy, the boyfriend attacked the woman when she walked into the house. Her brother was there and broke up the fight by hitting the boyfriend who was passed out and slumped over a table when the brother left. Later the boyfriend attacked the woman again, and this time she knocked him unconscious. After checking the children, she went to bed. Later the woman's five-year old girl went downstairs to go to the bathroom. The unemployed man returned from the party at 3:45am and found the five-year-old dead. She had been raped, severely beaten over most of her body and strangled to death by the boyfriend.

William Rowe, *quoted in the* Internet Encyclopedia of Philosophy

An example of animal suffering

In some distant forest lightning strikes a dead tree, resulting in a forest fire. In the fire a fawn is trapped, horribly burned, and lies in terrible agony for several days before death relieves its suffering.

William Rowe, The Problem of Evil and Some Varieties of Atheism, *1979*

Rowe's contention with these examples is that the five-year-old did not need to be raped and severely beaten before she was murdered if her *death* was necessary to bring about a greater good. All that was needed was for her to be killed quickly; and even this is open to doubt for the question is raised as to what greater good was achieved by this evil. Similarly the fawn could have died quickly rather than dying in terrible agony after several days for a greater good to be achieved. Rowe is arguing therefore that the evidence for unnecessary evil points to the non-existence of the God of classical theism.

Think about

Using the internet and/or library find out more about William Rowe's proposed evidential problem of evil and make your own notes about his views.

Activities

1. Write an explanation of the evidential problem of evil. In your explanation make sure that you include reference to the view of William Rowe.

2. List any objections that you can think of which a believer in the God of classical theism might provide to reject the problem of evil put forward by Hume.

3. Do you think that Hume and Rowe are right in stating that there is a problem for a believer? Give reasons for your opinion.

Religious responses to problem of evil

A typical defence against the problem of evil is that God's goodness is a very different concept from our own, and that as a temporary part of his plan his goodness might allow him to tolerate the existence of what we consider to be evil. If this is the case, there is no contradiction in supposing that God is all-loving, all-powerful *and* has a reason for allowing what we call evil to exist. A number of religious thinkers have constructed **theodicies** to explain what this reason might be.

What is a theodicy?

The term 'theodicy' literally means the 'justice of God', but when applied to the problem of evil it is better to think of it as 'the justification of God'. A theodicy is seeking to explain the apparent existence of evil in the world and at the same time to retain the three attributes of the God of classical theism of omnipotence, omnibenevolence and omniscience. Several theodicies have been developed to seek to resolve the problem of evil while retaining the goodness of God. These have included

Key terms

Theodicies: a theodicy is a defence of the justice of God in the light of evil. Theodicies generally argue that God is fair to allow the existence of evil and suffering because they are in some way necessary.

considering evil and suffering as an illusion. The theodicies that you are expected to be familiar with are:

- the theodicies in the Augustinian tradition
- the free will defence
- John Hick's 'vale of soul-making' theodicy (from the Irenaean tradition).

In this chapter we will also examine responses to evil in process thought which is regarded by many scholars not to be a theodicy as they consider it fails to retain the attributes of the God of classical theism within its explanation for the existence of evil.

Theodicies in the Augustinian tradition

There are several main themes in the theodicies in the **Augustinian tradition**. St Augustine (354–430) based his arguments on the Bible, in particular the Creation and Fall accounts in Genesis, and on philosophical tradition. His influential theodicy rests upon two major assumptions:

- Evil did not come from God since God's creation was faultless and perfect.
- Evil having come from elsewhere, God is justified in allowing it to stay.

St Augustine of Hippo

Augustine was converted to Christianity from **Manichaeism**, and the **Gnosticism** of this religion was to influence the way in which he developed his theodicy.

Manichaean theology teaches that two opposing natures existed from the beginning: light (good) and darkness (evil). A key belief in Manichaeism is that there is no omnipotent good power which is able to control this continual battle. Good has to fight an opponent with equal power to its own. In the theology, the human person is seen as a battleground for the power of light and darkness: the good part is the *soul* (which is composed of light) and the bad part is the *body* (composed of dark). The soul defines the person and is incorruptible, but it is under the domination of a foreign power, the body. Humans are said to be able to be saved from this power if they come to know who they are and identify themselves with their soul. Matter is evil and traps the human spirit, but within that human spirit there is some spark of the divine that must escape the material world to join the Ultimate Good. The true reality is not the world that people see around them but it is an immaterial world of being.

Augustine rejected the dualism of Manichaeism in favour of the God of classical theism, who has sovereignty over all things. However, although Augustine rejected Manichaeism, the influence on his theology can be seen in regard to the theodicy he developed to reconcile the existence of apparent evil with the God of classical theism. He has taken the Manichaeistic concept of the Good as that which brings tranquil pleasure and is linked to God's creation, and the dark becomes the evil which disrupts the harmony of the good creation. However, God preserves the order in his creation.

Wickedness and mortality are deemed to be both spiritually and physically evil in Manichaean terms because they disturb a person's tranquil existence; for Augustine these become 'sin' and the punishment for sin. Humans inherit sin as a punishment for the original sin of Adam and Eve and this can lead to spiritual blindness that causes the individual to turn away from God. Augustine's view that personal evil is inevitable was shared by the Manichees. However, Augustine assigned determination of one's destiny to the jurisdiction of God.

Augustine on predestination

Augustine claimed that God decided before He created the world who is to be saved and go to Heaven, and who is not and will go to hell. This decision was not based on a foreknowledge of the person's future acts, but on the unfailing wisdom of God. Augustine bases this conclusion on verses in the New Testament such as 'those God foreknew he also predestined to be conformed to the likeness of his Son' (Romans 8:28–30). Augustine thought that the number of the elect (those predestined for Heaven) was a fixed number that could not be changed.

Many scholars have challenged this view as it suggests that if God **predestines** some to Heaven and some to Hell, then God predestines some to sin. Augustine claimed that humans are not predestined to sin, but have free will to choose to sin and therefore can be held morally responsible for our sins.

Augustine's argument

The key themes of Augustine's theodicy may be summarised as follows:

- God is perfect. He made a world free from flaws.
- God cannot be blamed for creating evil since evil is not a substance but a **privation**, and it makes no sense to say that God created a privation.
- Evil comes from fallen angels and humans who chose deliberately to turn away from God.
- The possibility of evil in a created world is necessary. Only the uncreated God Himself can be perfect; created things are susceptible to change.
- Everybody is guilty because everyone was seminally present in the loins of Adam.
- Therefore everyone deserves to be punished.
- Natural evil is a fitting punishment and came about because the human action destroyed the natural order.
- Therefore God is right not to intervene and put a stop to suffering.
- That God saves some through Christ shows He is merciful as well as just.
- Augustine's aesthetic argument proposes that despite evil, the world is wholly good when it is viewed in its entirety.

Privatio boni

Augustine believed that God's love is incomprehensible and unchangeable, but it was out of this love that God created us. For Augustine, God is supreme perfection and goodness. God is the source of everything which, according to Augustine, was created by God out of nothing (*ex nihilo*). Therefore, Augustine argued, as everything in the world was created by God then it was created good and, perfect: free from defects. As God created everything then evil cannot be a thing. As God's creation was perfect then, at the time of creation, suffering and evil did not exist. In fact it would be impossible for evil to exist as the world and everything in it was God's creation and as God is perfect then God only creates perfect things. Augustine supported this argument by reference to Genesis 1:31, 'And God saw everything that he had made, and behold, it was very good'.

Take it further

Find out more about Manichaeism and the influence of the theology on Augustine.

Key terms

Predestines: in theology, predestination means being determined in advance; especially the doctrine (usually associated with Calvin) that God has foreordained every event throughout eternity (including the final salvation of mankind).

Privation: this occurs where something is lacking or missing. There is less of something. For example, in a famine there is a privation of food.

Think about

If God has predestined people, before they are born, to Heaven or Hell can it also be claimed that they have freedom of choice?

Activity

Read the accounts of Creation and the Fall in Chapters 1–3 of Genesis.

Link

If you are unsure about the differences between natural evil and moral evil, look back to p63.

Think about

Evil is the privation of good. It only applies to something that we would expect to be good by its nature. Is it a privation of goodness for cats not to have gills or snakes not to have legs? Is it a privation of goodness for people to commit murder?

According to Augustine, good is a substance whereas evil is not. God's creation was good and according to Augustine is still good: it is simply less good. There has been a privation of good (*privatio boni*), that is, evil is an absence of good. Augustine compared this to blindness as an absence of sight. Sight is a substance whereas blindness is a reduction in that substance. A privation is therefore a falling short of a thing's true nature. This means that everything considered evil must have some good in it. Augustine described the privation of goodness as:

> What, after all, is anything we call evil except the privation of good? In animal bodies, for instance, sickness and wounds are nothing but the privation of health. When a cure is effected, the evils which were present (that is, the sickness and the wounds) do not retreat and go elsewhere. Rather they simply do not exist any more. For such evil is not a substance; the wound or the disease is a defect of the bodily substance which, as a substance, is good. Evil then is an accident: that is a privation of the good which is called health. Thus, whatever defects there are in a soul are privations of a natural good. When a cure takes place, they are not transferred elsewhere, but since they are no longer present in the state of health, they no longer exist at all.

Augustine, Handbook on faith, hope and love, c.420

Everything in God's creation is good, but when people make the wrong choices then there is less good in the world.

Explanation for the origin of evil

Augustine traced the origin of evil to those areas within the world that have free will; namely, angels and human beings. These beings made wrong choices. However, as evil is not a substance they could not have chosen to do an evil thing. How, according to Augustine, did this privation of goodness occur? What was chosen was to turn their attention away from God, the Supreme Good, to things of lesser goodness.

> For when the will abandons what is above itself, and turns to what is lower, it becomes evil – not because that is evil to which it turns, but because the turning itself is wicked.

Augustine, City of God, c.426, 12:6

The fallen angels led by Lucifer chose to rebel against God and were cast out of Heaven. Adam and Eve disobeyed God by eating the forbidden fruit from the Tree of the Knowledge of Good and Evil and were cast out of the Garden of Eden. This misuse of free will unbalanced the harmony of God's creation and led to the privation of the goodness in the world that we call evil.

Explanation for the existence of suffering

Having explained the origin of evil, Augustine went on to show that all suffering is a fully deserved consequence of the human sin. The first sin caused the world to become distanced from God. In this new and damaged environment, remote from God, moral evil flourished and spread. Moral evil occurs because of the wrong choices that humans make when they disobey God's commands. For example, people ignore God's command, 'You shall not kill' or 'You shall not commit adultery' and as a result suffering occurs when murder or adultery occur.

Natural evil is the consequence of moral evil as the rebellion of the fallen angels and the first humans disrupted the perfect and natural order of God's creation. The disruption has prevented God's creation from achieving its true nature. Since original sin occurred, there has been enmity between humans and other creatures. Humans would have to battle constantly to grow enough food. Pain, such as that resulting from childbirth, entered the world, along with death.

Both types of evil are interpreted as a punishment: 'All evil is either sin or the punishment for sin.' Augustine made the essential point that *all* humans, including supposedly innocent babies, deserve to suffer because *all* humans were present 'in the loins of Adam'. This reflects the ancient belief that every generation was seminally present in Adam, and therefore that every generation is guilty because they inherit his guilt for disobeying God.

The principle of plenitude

There appears to be much inequality and unfairness in the world. Some creatures appear to have short harsh lives whereas others live long and happy ones. However, all occurrences in nature that we may regard as causing suffering to other creatures is not natural evil according to the **principle of plenitude**. Under this principle, within creation there must be the possibility of existence of every creation consistent with the nature of the world in which they are created. Augustine's view is that this diversity in the world is a good thing as by creating a world with such a range of things within them, God has created a perfect world as this diversity contributes to bringing about the perfection of the whole. Only God is capable of seeing the whole perspective of all things and therefore the goodness of the whole.

Augustine's aesthetics argument

Augustine concluded his theodicy with a reminder of God's grace: if God were simply just, everyone would go to his or her rightful punishment in Hell. Through God's grace Jesus was sent to die on the cross so that some might be saved and go to Heaven. This shows that God is merciful as well as just.

This strand of thought links to what is called Augustine's aesthetic argument. This states that the world only appears evil when sections of it are considered in isolation from the whole. But in the context of the final judgement, when evil will be punished, wrongs will be righted and God's astonishing grace will prevail, the totality of creation is good. Augustine therefore writes, 'the universe even with its sinister aspects is perfect' (*Soliloquies*, I, i, 2). He uses the analogy of a picture:

> For as the beauty of a picture is increased by well-managed shadows so, to the eye that has skill to discern it, the universe is beautified even by sinners, though, considered by itself, their deformity is a sad blemish.

Augustine, City of God, c.426, 11:23

The problem of evil can therefore be seen as a problem of perspective. Humans by their nature have a limited perspective, judging things by their practical usefulness to themselves and other self-centred criteria. From this point of view, evil is a reality. From the perspective of God's omniscience, however, evil has no reality, for what we consider evil in fact magnifies the goodness of the whole:

Key terms

Principle of plenitude: this asserts that everything that can happen will happen.

Think about

Augustine's theodicy is sometimes called the 'soul-deciding theodicy'. Why do you think it is given this title?

Activity

Write a 500–600-word explanation of Augustine's theodicy.

> To thee there is no such thing as evil, and even in thy whole creation taken as a whole, there is not; because there is nothing from beyond it that can burst in and destroy the order which thou hast appointed for it. But in parts of creation, some things, because they do not harmonise with others, are considered evil. Yet those same things harmonise with others and are good, and in themselves are good.

Augustine, Confessions, c.397, 7:13

Augustine gives the example of a scorpion's poison which is evil from its victim's point of view but not from the scorpion's point of view.

Developments of Augustine's theodicy

Augustine's theodicy had enormous influence on subsequent Christian thought. The following examples show some of the ways in which the main themes of his theodicy have been developed.

St Aquinas' development

St Thomas Aquinas developed a theodicy along the same lines as Augustine, the differences between the two being little more than refinements. Like Augustine, for example, he emphasises the nature of sin as a 'privation' or 'absence of good'. He traces all evil back to sin and the punishment of sin, which is an essential requirement of God's justice. He is keen to point out that, although in His omniscience God knew when He created the world that sin would be committed, He did not in any sense *determine* this to happen.

Interestingly, Aquinas acknowledges that God could have created a 'better' universe than ours (for example, by adding a greater number of beings), but crucially, this would be a different universe, and no longer ours. Accordingly, he argues that 'given the things which actually exist, the universe cannot be better' (Aquinas, *Summa Theologica*, I, xxv, 6). This is true despite the existence of sin, for like Augustine's aesthetic argument, Aquinas emphasises that this enhances the perfection of the whole world:

> God makes what is best in the whole, but not what is best in every single part, except in relation to the whole … And the whole itself, which is the universe of creatures, is all the better and more perfect if some things in it can fail in goodness, and do sometimes fail, God not preventing this … Hence many good things would be taken away if God permitted no evil to exist; for fire would not be generated if air was not corrupted, nor would the life of a lion be preserved unless an ass was killed. Neither would avenging justice nor the patience of a sufferer be praised if there were no injustice.

Aquinas, Summa Theologica, I, xlviii, 5

Take it further

Read the whole of Aquinas' development in the *Summa Theologica*, I, xlviii, 5.

This latter point suggests that evil has an instrumental value in developing human virtues such as patience. This theme is a central feature of the Irenaean tradition of theodicy that we will consider later.

John Calvin's development

John Calvin developed a number of Augustine's themes, but placed much greater reliance on the biblical teaching behind them, as opposed to philosophical arguments, such as about the nature of evil.

Human free will

Calvin places the blame for moral and natural evil entirely upon the shoulders of Adam who wilfully chose to abuse God's gift of free will and ignore the inclination towards good with which God had created him:

> Adam's choice of good and evil was free, and not that alone, but the highest rectitude was in his mind and will, and all the organic parts were rightly composed to obedience.
>
> ――
> *John Calvin*, Institutes of the Christian Religion, *1559, I, xv, 8*

As with Augustine, the original sin resulted in disaster:

> After the heavenly image was obliterated in him, he was not the only one to suffer this punishment – that, in place of wisdom, virtue, holiness, truth and justice ... there came forth the most filthy plagues, blindness, impotence, impurity, vanity, and injustice – but he also entangled and immersed his offspring in the same miseries ... All of us, who have descended from impure seed, are born infected with the contagion of sin.
>
> ――
> *John Calvin*, Institutes of the Christian Religion, *1559, II, i, 5*

As a result, man now sins 'willingly, not unwillingly or by compulsion'; by the most eager inclination of his heart, not by forced compulsion from without.

> ――
> *John Calvin*, Institutes of the Christian Religion, *1559, II, iii, 5*

■ **Link**

If you are not sure of what is meant by predestination look back at p69.

Predestination

Despite his emphasis upon human free will and blame, Calvin also argues that God predestined all of this to happen:

> We call predestination God's eternal decree, by which he determined with himself what he willed to become of each man. For all are not created in equal condition; rather eternal life is foreordained for some, eternal damnation for others. Therefore, as any man has been created to one or the other of these ends, we speak of him as predestined to life or to death.
>
> ――
> *John Calvin*, Institutes of the Christian Religion, *1559, III, xxi, 5*

Calvin also emphasises that the original sin of Adam was not just fore*known* but fore*ordained* or predetermined by God:

> God not only foresaw the fall of the first man, and in him the ruin of his descendants, but also meted it out in accordance with his own decision.
>
> ――
> *John Calvin*, Institutes of the Christian Religion, *1559, III, xxiii, 7*

He indeed explicitly rejects the view that God merely permits the sin:

> Why shall we say permission unless it is because God so wills? ... As if God did not establish the condition in which he wills the chief of his creatures to be.
>
> ――
> *John Calvin*, Institutes of the Christian Religion, *1559, III, xxiii, 8*

Done freely yet predestined?

Calvin is able to maintain that our actions are both determined and freely willed by adopting a particular understanding of free will, whereby a choice is freely willed as long as the agent desires it to happen, as opposed to being forced *against* his or her will. On this basis, Adam's sin was free because he wanted to commit it, even if it was determined that he would want to.

Although Calvin's doctrine of predestination raises serious questions about God's justice, in that it shows that God actively willed the damnation of many people, it can be seen as a necessary consequence of the Augustinian theme that God, in His grace, chose to save some of the sinners, for this entails that He did not choose to save the others. Moreover, Augustine accepted that when God created the world, He already knew that Adam would sin and which people He would choose to save. Some argue that the fact that God still went ahead with creation shows that He determined what followed. If this is true, Calvin is only making explicit a theme that was already implicit within Augustine's original argument.

To Calvin himself, there was not the faintest suggestion that predestination might threaten God's goodness, for this merely demonstrated God's total power and freedom. Calvin believed that because of their faults all punishment was fully deserved by humans. As with Augustine, the fact that despite this God still elected some to grace through no merit of their own was the clearest illustration of God's all-surpassing goodness.

Leibniz's development

In the 18th century, Leibniz developed Augustine's aesthetic argument into the main focus of his theodicy. He argued that our world is the best possible world, in that it permits the greatest quantity and variety of beings, resulting in the 'most reality, most perfection, most significance' possible. Faced with all of the possible universes that He could have created, God, being God, could not as Leibniz argued 'fail to act in the most perfect way, and consequently to choose the best' (*Monadology*, 1714).

Influence on the free-will defence

Of all of Augustine's themes, that which has formed the basis of more theodicies than any other is his emphasis upon human free will as the cause for moral evil. A number of different developments of this theme are explained in the section on the **free-will defence** below. However, as with many of his other themes it is worth pointing out that Augustine was not the *first* to use it as a basis of a theodicy. The free-will theme, for example, figured prominently in theodicies in the tradition of Irenaeus (*c*.130–202). The free-will defences can best be seen therefore as a development of a theme *used by* Augustine.

Think about

Augustine believed in both predestination and free will.

How is it possible to believe in both?

Activity

Write an explanation of Calvin's theodicy in your own words.

Key terms

Free-will defence: the view that human free will, and the context in which it can be meaningfully used, explain and justify the existence of evil in a world created by God.

Link

There is more about the free-will defence on pp79–82 and the influence of Irenaeus on pp83–85.

Activity

How convincing do *you* find Augustine's response to the problem of evil?

List both its strengths and weaknesses.

The strengths of Augustinian theodicies

Brian Davies supports the claim that evil cannot properly be called a substance and agrees that it is 'the gap between what there is and what there ought to be' (*An Introduction to Aquinas*, 2002). As such, we can agree with Augustine that evil is not a created entity but a privation of good. Any criticism of God would need to be based along the lines that God should somehow have created *more* than He has – which lacks precision. (It would be unclear *how much* more He should have created, for example.)

The view of Augustine and Aquinas that evil is less goodness as the result of human free will rather than an entity created by God can also be supported by the argument that if God gives human beings genuine free will, this *necessarily* entails the possibility of moral evil. Alvin Plantinga argues that although humans *sometimes* freely choose good, if God had designed them so that they would always choose good, they would not truly be free. Their 'choices' would be predetermined, like the 'decisions' made by robots.

The possibility of natural evil

Augustine's theodicy successfully accounts for the existence of natural evil as a result of the introduction of moral evil into the world. It can also be argued that if we are to have the genuine free will that Augustine assumes we have, there always needed to be the possibility of some natural evil. Without this possibility, for example, people would have less freedom to demonstrate courage and self-sacrifice in the face of real danger.

Many would support Augustine's assumption that free will is so valuable that it justifies the risk of evil. For without free will, humans would be as puppets or robots, and their humanity would be destroyed. Most religious believers would argue that people must turn to God out of their own free choice because otherwise the whole concept of religious faith would be meaningless.

Because of its compatibility with and reliance upon the Genesis account of Creation, Augustine's theodicy appeals to Christians who accept the authority of the Bible as the Word of God.

Heaven and Hell

In *The City of God*, Augustine called the Fall 'Oh happy fault' because Adam and Eve's original sin made it necessary for God to send Jesus. Augustine's theodicy is supported by the Christian belief that there will be a Judgement Day, when the good will go to Heaven and sinners will go to Hell. Because evil is punished, Augustine argued that God's world can still be seen as perfect in the end. Although all humans deserve the ultimate punishment of Hell, God offers forgiveness and salvation through belief in Jesus Christ enabling all who believe in Him to be saved.

Although the theme of predestination that was developed by Augustine and fully articulated by Calvin causes problems, it also has its strengths. It is supported by several biblical passages including Psalm 139:16: 'All the days ordained for me were written in your [God's] book before one of them came to be.' It is supported by God's omniscience and avoids the suggestion that evil either took God by surprise or frustrated His plans. It leaves intact the belief that God is completely in control of everything. Finally, for those who consider it is compatible with free will, it does not prevent God's punishment of humans from being fully deserved.

Link

Look back at Augustine's theme of predestination on p69 and Calvin's theme of predestination on pp73–74.

Activity

Christians believe that Hell is a place in which sinners are in isolation from God, without any hope of mercy or relief. For some Christians, especially during the time of Augustine, there would be physical torments as part of the punishment.

Using the internet and/or library, find out more on the different Christian beliefs about Hell and write a description of these beliefs.

The weaknesses of Augustinian theodicies

It has been argued that Augustine's theodicy contains logical, scientific and moral errors.

Logical errors

One logical problem has been expressed by F. D. E. Schleiermacher. He argued there was a logical contradiction in holding that a perfectly created world has gone wrong, since this would mean that evil has created itself out of nothing, which is logically impossible. Whether or not evil is a privation of good, it is still a real feature of the world, as is the suffering that it produces. As such, evil must somehow be attributed to God. Either the world was not perfect to begin with or God enabled it to go wrong.

Augustine was challenged as to why only some angels rebelled against God while others remained loyal and had to conclude:

> These angels, therefore, either received less of the grace of the divine love than those who persevered in the same; or if both were created equally good, then, while the one fell by their evil will, the others were more abundantly assisted, and attained to the pitch of blessedness at which they have become certain that they should never fall from it.

Augustine, City of God, c.426

This would suggest that there were flaws in God's creation if angels were not created equally good, and as a result of this flaw some angels were capable of rebellion. If God is omniscient then God must have known that the rebellion of the angels and the fall of Adam and Eve would occur yet did nothing to stop it. Therefore God is ultimately responsible for the reduction of good in His creation.

Augustine's appeal to the free-will defence poses a logical difficulty within the specific framework of his theodicy. It is hard to see how, in a perfect world where there was no knowledge of good and evil, there could possibly be freedom to obey or disobey God, since good and evil would be unknown. The fact that God's creatures chose to disobey Him seems to suggest there was already knowledge of evil, which could only have come from God. On the other hand if there is to be real free will then there has to be the ability to commit sins, the opportunity to commit sins and, paradoxically, the permission to commit sins. If God has not allowed all three then many scholars claim that free will would only be an illusion.

A further logical difficulty can best be seen in Calvin's development of Augustine's theodicy. This is the problem that if, as Calvin argued, humans are predestined by God, there are good grounds for saying that they cannot truly be free in the sense of being morally responsible for the Fall. In which case, it would be incoherent to appeal to the free-will defence to justify evil. This argument focuses on the relationship between free will and determinism and is considered more fully in the section on moral errors below.

Scientific errors

With the exception of Leibniz, the Augustine theodicy depends on a literal interpretation of Genesis 3 that Adam and Eve committed the original sin of disobeying God by eating the forbidden fruit. John Hick argues that Augustian theodicy is flawed because it:

> is fatally lacking in plausibility. For most educated inhabitants of the modern world regard the biblical story of Adam and Eve, and their

■ **Take it further**

Use the internet to find out more about F. D. E. Schleiermacher's argument that there was a logical contradiction in holding that a perfectly created world has gone wrong.

■ **Think about**

■ How do *you* know that certain laws should not be broken?

■ What is the problem with holding that, in a world which has no knowledge of good or evil, God uttered the command not to eat a particular fruit?

■ **Link**

Look back to Chapter 1, p15 and remind yourself of the importance of the philosopher John Hick.

temptation by the devil, as myth rather than as history, and they believe that so far from having been created finitely perfect and then falling, humanity evolved out of lower forms of life, emerging in a morally, spiritually, and culturally primitive state. Further they reject as incredible the idea that earthquake and flood, disease, decay, and death are consequences either of a human fall, or of a prior fall of angelic beings who are now exerting an evil influence upon the earth. They see all this as part of a pre-scientific world view.

John Hick, quoted in S. T. Davis (ed.), Encountering Evil: Live Options in Theodicy, *2001*

These scientific difficulties stem from the Augustinian reliance upon the Genesis Creation and Fall stories. As a result, much of the argument rests upon ancient and scientifically controversial Judaeo-Christian theology. This dependence leads to two major criticisms:

■ One problem is Augustine's idea that the world was made perfect by God and then damaged by humans. This contradicts evolutionary theory, which asserts that the universe has continually been developing from an earlier stage of chaos. Essential to evolution, moreover, is the innate and selfish desire for survival. This renders the Genesis concept of blissful happiness in the Garden of Eden still less easy to accept. Yet if God's world contained flaws at the outset, God must bear responsibility for evil.

■ The second major weakness concerns Augustine's assumption that each human being was seminally present in Adam. This theory must be rejected on biological grounds, which means that we are not in fact guilty for Adam's sin. This means, of course, that God is not just in allowing us to suffer for someone else's sin.

Moral errors

A serious moral problem concerns Augustine's view that God graciously forgives some sinners and calls them to eternal life in Heaven. The problem is that since everyone deserves punishment, God is arbitrarily favouring some over others and showing irrational inconsistency. If He is able to save some, He could have saved others, and the fact that He does not suggests that He cannot be *all*-loving.

A further problem concerns Augustine's view that God chose to create the world despite knowing that the Fall would happen. John Hick argues that this must make God ultimately responsible for evil. Given that we would hold a manufacturer responsible for knowingly making a faulty product, God must be held to account for the sinfulness of humans. It can be argued that God is far more responsible, for His omnipotence suggests that He could have found a way to avoid the fault. Augustine's theodicy therefore fails in its claim that evil is the punishment we deserve, for the punishment is unwarranted.

This moral problem is seen most clearly in Calvin's doctrine of predestination, but Hick argues that this only makes clear what was already implicit in Augustine's theodicy. It therefore reveals a serious weakness in the whole tradition. The act of deliberately creating people so that they will spend eternity in Hell is an act of torture that is totally at odds with love, and still less the will of an all-loving God. The very existence of Hell demonstrates that evil and punishment are written into the design of the universe.

The compatibility of determinism with free will

Calvin's claim that divine determinism is compatible with free will is heavily criticised. Kant described this concept as a 'miserable subterfuge' and William James as a 'quagmire of evasion'. It can be argued that to blame a human being for performing willingly the acts that were determined for him makes no more sense than blaming a computer for being badly programmed.

Kant accepted that there is determinism in the empirical world or world of appearances, and freedom in the world of things-in-themselves, the world of reason, but could not accept that we would have any freedom if there was divine determinism and the action was predetermined. Kant uses the example of a thief to support his point.

> If I say of a human being who commits a theft that this deed is, in accordance with the natural law of causality, a necessary result of determining grounds in preceding time, then it was impossible that it could have been left undone; how, then, can appraisal in accordance with the moral law make any change in it and suppose that it could have been omitted because the law says that it ought to have been omitted? That is, how can that man be called quite free at the same point of time and in regard to the same action in which and in regard to which he is nevertheless subject to an unavoidable natural necessity?
>
> *Kant*, Critique of Pure Reason, 1781

In such situations Kant did not believe it was possible to consider the individual as free and described this concept as a 'miserable subterfuge'.

In his article *Doctrine of Determinism*, William James considers that determinism is a 'quagmire of evasion under which the real issue of fact has been entirely smothered', and for James, 'freedom presents no problem at all'. For James, we must have the possibilities of making our own moral choices.

> Whether the creator leave the absolute chance possibilities to be decided by himself, each when its proper moment arrives, or whether, on the contrary, he alienate this power from himself, and leave the decision out and out to finite creatures such as we men are. The great point is that the possibilities are really here. Whether it be we who solve them, or he working through us, at those soul trying moments when fate's scales seem to quiver, and good snatches the victory from evil or shrinks nerveless from the fight, is of small account, so long as we admit that the issue is decided nowhere else than here and now.
>
> *William James*, The Will to Believe and Other Essays in Popular Philosophy, 1897

■ Link

Look back to p74 to remind yourself how Augustine's theodicy has influenced the development of the free-will defence.

However, if to avoid this problem it is conceded that God did not determine human beings and did not know that they would commit sins, then His omniscience is challenged along with His omnipotence, for this would suggest that God failed to create the perfect world that He intended to. The existence of Hell as a place of eternal suffering would then merely demonstrate the extent to which his plans had been turned upside down.

Augustine's aesthetic argument raises further difficulties. One is that even if the world were considered good as a whole, the fact remains that humans do not have this all-encompassing vision. To them, suffering is a terrible reality. It would be of no comfort, for example, to tell a person dying from a poisonous bite that the poison is good in itself. If it were truly good in itself, it should not cause an agonising death. A second problem is that if human sin really did contribute to the overall goodness of the world, there would be still less justification for God to punish the entire human race for introducing it to the world.

The combined effect of these criticisms leads most people to conclude that Augustine's theodicy does not work.

The free-will defence

One of the key themes in Augustine's theodicy is the idea that evil is the result of human free will rather than God's will. This theme has been developed into a theodicy in its own right called the free-will defence (FWD). The free-will defence argues as a starting point that free will is an essential part of humanity, without which we would be mere robots. This explains why free will is sufficiently important to be worth the risk of evil. Secondly it argues that genuine free will requires the genuine possibility of evil, so that if God has removed this possibility He would have to have taken away our free will. Then it argues that even the terrible extent of evil throughout history is in some way necessary to our free will, explaining why God does not simply step in and rescue us from the worst effects of our choices.

The free-will defence centres on the idea that for humans to respond freely to God, without which no genuine relationship with Him would be possible, they must be able to make their own decisions and choose to love God of their own free will. This means that, ultimately, humans must have the choice to do good or to commit evil. When moral evil occurs, it is because humans have misused their God-given freedom. The free will defence attempts to combat the problem of evil by rationalising that evil is the result of human action and therefore God is not to be held accountable for it.

The philosopher Søren Kierkegaard used the parable of the king and the peasant girl to support free-will defence. In the outline of the parable that follows the king represents God, and the peasant girl, humanity. A rich king fell in love with a peasant girl. He decided to draw up a royal decree that would force her to marry him. But the king realised that if he forced her to marry him, he would never be really sure of her love. Then he considered that if he appeared to her in his finest clothes and showed his great wealth and power she would agree to become his wife. But he realised that he would never know if she had married him for his riches and power. Finally the king decided that he would go and live and work with the villagers as a peasant and seek to win the girl as his wife. Only then, if she had fallen in love with him as himself, could he be sure that she really loved him.

Swinburne's support for free will

This leaves the question why God, if He is omnipotent and omniscient, could not intervene to prevent at least the most serious effects of moral evil. Richard Swinburne argues that the reason why God cannot intervene to stop suffering is that this would jeopardise human freedom and take away the need for responsibility and development. Swinburne argues that God cannot intervene even when such moral evil occurs as the death of six million Jews during the Holocaust, as such intervention would compromise human freedom. If God is to give humanity freedom then God can never intervene otherwise there is not total freedom of choice.

Think about

Do you think that the criticisms of the Augustinian theodicies are justified? Support your views with evidence.

Activity

Read the outline of Søren Kierkegaard's parable of the king and the peasant girl. Explain how this parable supports the free-will defence.

Take it further

Using the internet and/or library read the entire parable of Søren Kierkegaard.

Nazis arresting Jews in the Warsaw Ghetto

> The less he allows men to bring about large scale horrors, the less the freedom and responsibility he gives them. We are … asking that God should make a toy world, a world where things matter, but not very much; where we can choose and our choices can make a small difference but the real choices remain God's. For he simply would not allow us the choice of doing real harm … He would be like an over-protective parent who will not let his child out of sight for a moment.

Richard Swinburne, The Existence of God, *1992*

Activity

How convincing do you find the free-will defence to the problem of evil?

List both its strengths and weaknesses.

It can be argued that even though God is omnipotent, He can only do that which is logically possible; and it would not be logically possible for God to take away evil and suffering while granting us true free will.

The strengths of the free-will defence

The free-will defence provides a logical reason for the existence of moral evil in the world and removes the blame from God by placing it on humanity.

Modern philosophers generally support the view that if God gives human beings genuine free will, this *necessarily* entails the possibility of moral evil. Mackie had taken the opposite view, arguing that God could have created humans so that they had freedom of choice, yet still always *chose* good. However, Plantinga agrees with Hick that although humans *sometimes* freely choose good, if God had *designed* them so that they would *always* choose good, they would not truly be free. Their 'choices' would be predetermined, like the 'decisions' made by robots.

There is support also for the view that the benefits of free will are sufficient to justify the inherent risk of evil. In addition, free will brings for Christians the greatest reward of all: unity with God in Heaven. The Christian tradition has argued that by following the teaching and example of Jesus, it is possible to achieve God's forgiveness for sin and to form an eternal relationship with him. This can only be achieved through the individual's free choice:

> If my people, who are called by my name, will humble themselves and pray and seek my face and turn from their wicked ways, then will I hear from heaven and will forgive their sin and will heal their land.

2 Chronicles 7:14

Although the free-will defence is generally thought only to account for moral evil, it can also account for some types of natural evil. Swinburne took the example of death and argued that, despite the suffering it causes, it is nevertheless essential to the free-will defence. This is because death means that life, and the chances that each life contains, are limited. This is vital, because only in a limited lifespan can we have genuine responsibility for our actions:

> A situation of temptation with infinite chances is no situation of temptation at all. If there is always another chance there is no risk. There would not be overriding reasons not to do a bad act, if you are always preserved from its consequences … If you cannot damn yourself no matter how hard you go on trying, your salvation will be inevitable … a God who wishes that all men shall be saved is a being of dubious moral status.

Richard Swinburne, The Existence of God, 1992

In other words, if we were immortal there would always be another chance for us to make amends and so probably that would never happen. The world therefore needs to contain natural laws which can cause death, however painful this may be.

Death also limits the time during which an individual is able to inflict suffering on others, meaning that there is a sense in which it can be seen as merciful.

> There must be limits to the intensity of suffering. A natural death after a certain small finite number of years provides the limit to the period of suffering. It is a boundary to the power of an agent against another agent. For death removes agents from that society of interdependent agents in which it is good that they should play their part.

Richard Swinburne, The Existence of God, 1992

The free-will defence is therefore able to explain death and perhaps other natural evils that are necessary to facilitate death. To this extent it can justify the suffering caused.

The weaknesses of the free-will defence

Peter Vardy notes that a major criticism of the free-will defence is that it fails to explain the existence of natural evil in the world. Natural evil such as floods and disease is often independent of any actions of humans and cannot be controlled by them. It is true that Swinburne has argued that natural evils like death can have a part to play in making our free will more meaningful, but William Rowe has shown that there are many examples of natural evil that do not produce any such greater good for anyone. So God is not freed from the responsibility for natural evil. Alvin Plantinga has argued that neither God nor humans are responsible for these things, but that fallen angels are their cause. Many, however, would reject the whole concept of such beings.

■ Link

Reread William Rowe's examples of natural evil on p66.

J. L. Mackie undermines one of the most basic assumptions of the free-will defence: that free will entails the potential for evil. Mackie suggests that God could have created a world in which humanity has freedom of choice but always chooses good:

> If there is no logical impossibility in a man's freely choosing the good on one, or on several occasions, there cannot be a logical impossibility in his freely choosing the good on every occasion. God was not, then, faced with a choice between making innocent automata and making beings who, in acting freely, would sometimes go wrong: there was open to him the obviously better possibility of making beings who would act freely but always go right. Clearly, his failure to avail himself of this possibility is inconsistent with his being both omnipotent and wholly good.
>
> *J. L. Mackie*, 'Evil and Omnipotence', Mind, *April 1955*

If this challenge is true, then God's gift of free will cannot excuse the existence of evil, for God could simply have made morally superior free beings who would never wish to sin and who would never have caused so much suffering. Mackie concludes that since God did not do this, He cannot be omnipotent and all-loving.

The free-will defence comes under fire from **determinists** who argue that every human choice and action is nothing more than the effect of a prior cause. This is a major threat because, if our lives are determined by events outside our control, it can be argued that our 'freedom' is an illusion anyway, and so cannot justify suffering.

The belief that God is omniscient itself suggests that we are determined. If everything is created by God, and God knows in advance everything that His creation will do, God would seem to have deliberately determined evils like the Holocaust. If, on the other hand, God had no idea what would happen, then His omnipotence and omniscience would seem to be eroded.

Irenaeus attacked Gnosticism in his work *Refutation of Heresies*. Most important was his rejection of the Gnostic belief that there were two forces working and that as the world is material God had not made it. He also rejected their teaching that Jesus had brought two doctrines, one doctrine that was available to everyone, and one doctrine that was only for the spiritually elite, which included the Gnostics. Irenaeus believed that the Gospel message is for everyone.

■ Key terms

Determinists: people who accept the philosophical doctrine that every state of affairs, including every human event, act and decision has already been decided (determined), for example, by God.

AQA Examiner's tip

Remember when asked to assess a philosophical question that you need to consider both the strengths and weaknesses of the arguments put forward, and reach a conclusion.

■ Link

If you are uncertain about the meaning of the term 'Gnosticism' look back at p68.

Activities

1   Write an essay in answer to the following:

Assess the claim that the free-will defence adequately explains the existence of evil in the world created by God.

2   Read the sections below relating to Hick's modern presentation of the Irenaean theodicy.

Write an explanation of why it is not possible to accept both Gnostic teaching and this theodicy?

John Hick's 'vale of soul-making' theodicy

Hick's vale of soul-making theodicy is a modern presentation of the **Irenaean theodicy**. This argues that both natural and moral evil are essential to 'soul-making' so they have a good purpose. An all-loving God is therefore justified in making a world such as this and in allowing humanity to perform evil acts. Irenaeus and Augustine both traced evil back to human free will, but where Augustine considered evil to be totally at odds with God's purposes, Irenaeus thought it had a valuable part to play within His plans for humans. Hick develops this theme into a fuller explanation of the importance and implications of evil for both God and humans. Hick's argument is known as the vale of soul-making theodicy.

The central features of Hick's theodicy

Hick argues that instead of creating humans as morally perfect beings from the outset, God deliberately left them imperfect or 'unfinished' to enable them to complete the process of creation themselves. Following Irenaeus, he argued that humans are created as children of God in the *image of God* with the potential to achieve perfection in the future, when they will be in the *likeness of God*.

Irenaeus' view was that man as a personal and moral being already exists in the image, but has not yet been formed into the finite likeness, of God. By this 'likeness' Irenaeus means something more than personal existence as such; he means a certain valuable quality of personal life which reflects finitely the divine life. This represents the perfecting of man, the fulfilment of God's purpose for humanity, the 'bringing of many sons to glory', the creating of 'children of God' who are 'fellow heirs with Christ' of his glory (Hick, Evil and Soul-Making, http://mind.ucsd.edu/syllabi/02-03/01w/readings/hick.html).

Evil as the means through which humans become 'children of God'

If this 'likeness' is to be achieved then Hick has to admit that this makes God partly responsible for the evil in the world as it is the means through which humans will become 'children of God'. However, he argues that God had a sufficiently good reason for allowing evil that its existence does not threaten His perfectly loving nature. God *needed* to allow humans to develop themselves rather than creating them perfectly, because virtues that have been formed as a result of a person overcoming temptations and challenges are 'intrinsically more valuable than virtues created within him ready made without effort on his own part' (Hick, quoted in S. T. Davis (ed.), *Encountering Evil: Live Options in Theodicy*, 2001). For example, if God wanted humans to be *genuinely* loving, He had to give them the opportunity to develop this quality for themselves. If we had been created so that we would always automatically love and obey God, we would have been robots and our 'love' would have been meaningless. As the free-will defence has established, if we are to have genuine free choice, evil must be both a possibility and, to some extent, a reality.

Evil is undeniably unpleasant, but it is an essential part of the development of moral perfection, which Hick describes as 'soul-making'. No suffering in the Irenaean tradition is pointless. There is therefore a sense in which by allowing evil (which is contrary to His nature) to exist in His creation, God is in fact demonstrating the true extent of His love for humans.

Key terms

Irenaean theodicy: theodicies in this tradition follow the lead of the 2nd-century bishop now Saint Irenaeus. The key theme of the theodicy is that humanity develops through encountering evil, so evil has a good purpose. Following Hick, this is also known as the soul-making theodicy.

Think about

The Augustinian theodicy is often called the 'soul-deciding' theodicy. Why do you think John Hick's theodicy is called the 'vale of soul-making' theodicy?

Take it further

- Using the internet and/or library find out more about the theodicy of Irenaeus from which Hick developed his 'vale of soul-making' theodicy.
- List the ways in which the two theodicies are similar and ways in which they are different.

Link

Reread the explanation of the free-will defence (see pp79–80) to remind yourself why free will requires the possibility of evil and why it is so valuable as to justify the risk of evil.

Hick develops his theodicy by examining the type of creation that God needed to bring about if it were to be the best environment for the process of soul-making.

God is at an epistemic distance

Hick argues that God could have created humanity directly in His presence so that they were automatically aware of His limitless divine power. However, if God had done this then the gap between God and humanity would be so small that the latter would have no freedom in relation to God.

God has therefore chosen the better course which is to place humanity at sufficient distance to have awareness but not certainty of God.

> In order to be a person, exercising some measure of genuine freedom, the creature must be brought into existence, not in the immediate divine presence, but at a distance from God.

John Hick, Encountering Evil: Live Options in Theodicy, *1982*

Key terms

Epistemic distance: a distance in the dimension of knowledge.

Counterfactual hypothesis: this is the method of enquiry that examines what would happen if a situation had been brought about in a different way to that in which it was.

This is not a spatial distance but an **epistemic distance**. An epistemic distance means that there is a knowledge gap between God and humans. Humans are not born with the innate knowledge of God's existence and have to seek God through faith. Humans are able to exist as finite beings with the freedom of choice as to whether they acknowledge and worship, or turn away from, God.

> Humanity is created at an epistemic distance from God in order to come freely to know and love their Maker; and that they are at the same time created as morally immature and imperfect beings in order to attain through freedom the most valuable quality of goodness.

John Hick, Encountering Evil: Live Options in Theodicy, *1982*

Think about

■ Imagine that wherever you drive in your car, the Chief of Police accompanies you.

■ Are you still free to break the speed limit?

■ Would you, in practice, exceed it?

The argument is that were God's presence to be too imminent, humans would be overwhelmed by knowledge of God's expectations. In practice, therefore, they would obey God not because they had chosen to upon their own volition, but because He was overlooking their every move.

Why is the world not a paradise?

Hick further argues that natural evil has a part to play in the process of soul-making. For if the world were a paradise, where there were no possible chance of ever causing any kind of harm, humans would not in fact be free, because every possible human action would result in happiness. Evil would be indistinguishable from good since both would result in the same thing. Consequently, humans would in effect be robots and not, in fact, humans. A further and related argument for the presence of real, actual evil is that without such evil, everyone would follow God's laws because there would never be any difficulty in doing so. Qualities such as courage, honour and love would all be impossible. As a result, there would be no opportunity to develop into God's likeness, and since these qualities are essential to such development then there need to be opportunities to achieve them in this world.

In this case, the **counterfactual hypothesis** establishes that God's purpose would not be possible in a world completely free from suffering and evil. God therefore chose to create an imperfect world to give humans the chance to develop real virtues by overcoming its difficulties and temptations. This development occurs by not only avoiding the temptation to commit moral evil oneself and dealing with the challenges that occur when others commit it, but also by coping with the evil and suffering resulting from natural evil.

Hick therefore argues that the world has to be one containing:

> unpredictable contingencies and dangers – in which unexpected and undeserved calamities may occur to anyone – because only in such a world can mutual caring and love be elicited.

John Hick, Encountering Evil: Live Options in Theodicy, *1982*

He concludes that since our world offers these opportunities for 'moral growth and development', which would not be available in a pain-free world, it is the best world in which to develop. Accordingly he describes it as the 'vale of soul-making'.

So, while it may not be possible to demonstrate the need for every individual example of suffering, the world must contain natural laws which can produce some suffering. Therefore, Hick concludes that while our world is not:

> designed for the maximisation of human pleasure and the minimisation of human pain, it may nevertheless be rather well adapted to the quite different purpose of 'soul making'.

John Hick, Philosophy of Religion, *1990*

Hick does not believe that this process towards the *likeness of God* is 'completed in the life of the individual' except for a small minority that are recognised as saints. It is therefore completed in the afterlife. All will eventually become the 'children of God' and 'inherit eternal life'.

The need for an afterlife

The final element of Hick's theodicy concerns the importance of the afterlife. There are three reasons for this:

- The process towards the likeness of God is rarely 'completed in the life of the individual' except for a small minority that are recognised as saints. The challenges of the world do not always result in genuine human development. If life were to end at death, God's original purpose for creation would have been frustrated.

- Only a supremely good future in Heaven can justify the magnitude of the suffering endured.

- Many apparently 'evil' people are nothing more than 'victims of the system'; people who perhaps have been brought up badly and who cannot be held totally responsible for their actions. It would threaten God's justice if these people were overlooked by not being given a place in Heaven.

It is therefore essential to Hick's theodicy that *all people* will eventually become the 'children of God' and 'inherit eternal life'.

Think about

- Can evil or suffering ever be valuable?
- Consider some examples of evil and suffering, perhaps where *you* suffered. Are there any occasions where you can see that the evil and suffering has resulted in good in the longer term?

Activity

Write a 500–600-word explanation of Hick's soul-making theodicy.

Think about

Why do you think many people find Irenaeus' theodicy more credible than that of Augustine? Consider, for example, how Irenaeus allows room for the modern concept of evolution and avoids Augustine's stumbling block of evil appearing from nowhere.

Take it further

Read Irenaeus, *Against Heresies*, iv, xxxix.1.

The strengths of Hick's theodicy

Hick's theodicy is supported by a well-established Christian tradition dating back to Irenaeus. Irenaeus argued that without evil, good would have no meaning; 'How, if we had no knowledge of the contrary, could we have instruction in that which is good?' (Irenaeus, *Against Heresies*, iv, xxxix.1). Without the contrast between good and evil, humans would be robots rather than morally free beings:

> If anyone do shun the knowledge of both kinds of things ... he unaware divests himself of the character of a human being.

Irenaeus, Against Heresies, c.180, iv, xxxix.1

Link

Look back at p79 and remind yourself of Søren Kierkegaard's parable of the king and the peasant girl.

Think about

Do you agree with Gil Edwards that it is only through suffering that qualities such as courage and trust can come to the fore? What are the reasons for your opinion?

Think about

■ Consider why *you* are studying philosophy of religion.

■ Why do your teachers not simply answer the exam questions for you, and give you a copy of the answers?

■ What is the difference between this situation and Hick's argument that the omnipotent God needed to allow humans to develop for themselves?

In *Stepping into the Magic* Gil Edwards argues that it is only through suffering that qualities such as courage, trust, tolerance and integrity have an opportunity to come to the fore. This supports Hick's argument that evil is essential to the process of soul-making.

Peter Vardy uses the analogy of the king who falls in love with a peasant girl to support Hick's argument that God needed to allow humans to develop themselves rather than creating them perfect, because goodness that has been developed by free choice is infinitely better than the programmed reliability of robots. Vardy points out that although the king could have forced the girl to marry him, he chose instead to win her round of her own accord since love cannot be created by compulsion. In the same way, God had to allow humans to love and obey Him for themselves if their love for Him was to be genuine.

If we accept that human perfection must be developed rather than ready-made, then other aspects of Hick's theodicy must also be accepted. For if we are to be able to develop:

■ we had to be created imperfect

■ we had to be distanced from God

■ the natural world could not be a paradise.

The theodicy therefore provides a rational explanation for why the God of classical theism who is omnipotent, omniscient and omnibenevolent permits both natural and moral evil and the resulting suffering. It also has the advantage over Augustine's theodicy that it is in line with the scientific theory of evolution as humans are developing from one stage into another and there is no insistence upon a former period of perfection.

The weaknesses of Hick's theodicy

Hick's theodicy has the concept that everyone will go to Heaven and this seems unjust. Those who accept Hick's principle that evil can assist with human development often criticise his theodicy for failing to justify the extent and severity of suffering in the world. Regarding the Holocaust, for example, would it not have been sufficient for four million Jews to die instead of six million? Likewise, even if it is accepted that the counter-factual hypothesis demonstrates that soul-making could not take place in a paradise, does it really need to be plagued with such excessive natural earthquakes as the Indian Ocean tsunami? To the extent that such excessive suffering is pointless, it is therefore unjustifiable. Supporters of the theodicy would reply that they have missed the key message that no suffering is pointless as it all provides an opportunity for human development.

Within this approach natural evils provide opportunities for the exercise of morally good behaviour which, encourage through humans cooperating with each other, the outpouring of good moral actions which move humanity further toward the possession of God's likeness.

Peter Manning, God, Evil and the Big Wave, Dialogue *magazine, issue 24*

It also appears that the suffering of some is used for the benefit of others' development and this would suggest that God thinks more highly of some people than others. This suggestion that God uses some people and situations as a means of allowing others to develop has been regarded as racist by some black theologians. A response to this criticism would be that it is not God who chose to take black Africans into slavery or to seek to eliminate the Jews but humans, and if God has given humans total freedom to choose what is right or wrong then God cannot interfere. Hick argues that if God is going to give humanity freedom it would be a contradiction for God to interfere. Hick considers that there would be no point in God creating finite humans unless they have genuine freedom to act independent of God. And as a result of giving humanity this freedom then God cannot guarantee that humans will always use their freedom to act in a moral way with each other.

Hick's theodicy is also unable to explain why suffering is distributed so inconsistently; with some people suffering enormously and others very little. If suffering is as essential to human development as Hick suggests, it is surely unfair that some people miss out on its benefits! However, if they can develop in other ways, then surely everyone could have done so too. This again suggests that the excessive suffering that so many experience is unnecessary.

A related problem is that Hick's theodicy fails to account for animal suffering. How is it justifiable for animals to suffer if it is only humans who benefit from pain? Again Hick would respond by pointing out that such events result from the workings of natural laws provided for the purposes of soul-making.

Think about

Anthony Pinn in his book *Why, Lord? — Suffering and Evil in Black Theology*, challenges Hick's theodicy on the grounds that if we expect God to generate good from evil then it stops individuals challenging evils in society such as racism. Pinn thinks that the idea that suffering can be redemptive lessens the recognition that evil is completely evil. Do you agree with Pinns' point? What are the reasons for your view?

Take it further

Find out more about why many black theologians find it difficult to accept Hick's 'vale of soul-making theodicy'.

Why do animals suffer?

Suffering does not express God's love

A more fundamental criticism is the view that suffering can never be an expression of God's love. It can be argued that love can never be expressed by allowing any amount of suffering, no matter what the reason. D. Z. Phillips argued that it would never be justifiable to hurt someone in order to help them. When we consider the magnitude of suffering in our world, this problem is all the more serious.

Scholars who support Hick's theodicy would respond by pointing out that these critics have missed the point of the soul-making theodicy. It is teleological (*teleos* is a Greek word meaning 'end' or 'purpose'). God's purpose for humanity is soul-making so that everyone can achieve the reward of becoming 'children of God'. However, the character, Ivan Karamazov in Fyodor Dostoyevsky's novel *The Brothers Karamazov* refuses to believe in a God who allows innocent children to suffer. He emphasises that such suffering can never be justified, even by the promise of eternal compensation in Heaven.

Mary Midgely expresses concern that Hick does not take into account human wickedness in creating evil and suffering seriously. Midgely believes that the examination of evil as a positive trait is misguided, as by suggesting that God is ultimately responsible for allowing evil then it does not highlight sufficiently our responsibility for much moral evil. The focus should be on humanity and what makes people wicked as she sees evil as our problem not God's. If God has made us capable of committing evil then we need to understand what it is so that we can control it. She believes that the problem of evil is not just about why God allows evil but discovering why humans have natural tendencies towards what she calls 'wickedness', in order to combat them.

Many Christians are concerned that Hick's theodicy is inconsistent with the role of Jesus as saviour. Jesus' role is no longer the innocent sacrifice to gain God's forgiveness for original sin, as in this theodicy Adam and Eve are not the cause of evil entering the world. Jesus' role becomes one of teacher and an example of how to lead a moral life.

Finally, Hick's view that everyone will go to Heaven has attracted criticism because it does not seem fair and therefore calls God's justice into question. Religious people object to it because it contradicts religious texts including the Bible and Qur'an which promise punishment for the unrighteous. It also makes moral behaviour pointless; if everyone is to be rewarded with Heaven, what is the point of going out of our way to do good? We are left with no incentive to make the development that Hick regards as so important, because we know that it will happen eventually anyway.

Is free will a satisfactory explanation?

The theodicies of Augustine and Hick, as well as the free-will defence, all appeal to the role of human free will in their justification of evil. For Augustine, free will explains the Fall on the grounds that if we are completely free, the risk of sin is unavoidable. Similarly the free-will defence argues that without freedom of choice then we are no more than robots and that freedom of choice entails the risk of evil. Hick focuses on the reasons why God chose to give us such freedom; namely, so that we might develop to perfection. This appeal to free will explains not only moral evil but also some natural evil, through such arguments as the counterfactual hypothesis.

Think about

Do you think Mary Midgely is right and that attempts to explain why God allows evil distract people from finding out how to stop people from committing acts of wickedness? Why do you hold this view?

Think about

- If you had known, at school, that no matter what you did with your time you were going to gain the top grades in every exam, how would your behaviour have differed?

- If this had been the case, clearly you would have been unpopular with friends. Why might you yourself not have benefited from guaranteed success?

Link

Reread the quotation from Mackie's argument on p82 and the explanation that follows it. How convincing do you find his argument?

Think about

Why do you think that many philosophers consider Mackie's criticism to be invalid?

The strengths and weaknesses of the appeal to free will have already been considered in the critiques of Augustine, the free-will defence and Hick. One of the strongest arguments that free will is not a satisfactory explanation for evil in a world created by God came from J. L. Mackie, who claimed that God could have created a race of genuinely free beings who would never have chosen to commit evil. If this is accepted as valid, it threatens to undermine all three theodicies.

If free will is God's gift, it still cannot excuse the existence of evil, for God could simply have made morally superior free beings who would never wish to sin and who would never have caused so much suffering. Mackie concludes that since God did not do this, He cannot be omnipotent and all-loving.

In addition to Alvin Plantinga's argument against Mackie, John Hick argued that while humans might have *appeared* to be freely choosing the good on all occasions, in relation to God they would not be free because God would have made them in such a way that He knew they would never choose evil. From God's point of view, therefore, such humans would be no more satisfying than robots because their future choices were already known when they were made.

> John Hick argues that the emergence of humanity through evolution enhances human freedom as we do not feel constrained by God's will. In an evolutionary world in which the existence of God is not always obvious, to discover and to live out the will of God, has greater value in the journey of the soul-making that moves humanity towards attaining the likeness of God, than if things were easier.
>
> *Peter Manning*, God, Evil and the Big Wave, Dialogue *magazine, issue 24*

If God did not create the world, then free-will defence fails. To decide whether or not free will provides a satisfactory explanation for the existence of evil in the world created by God, it is necessary to weigh up the strengths and weaknesses of each response to the problem of evil and reach your own conclusion. For example, you could balance the arguments about the benefits of free will for human development and the need for God to allow us to face the consequences of our choices, with Rowe's argument that evil is often pointless and Phillip's view that it cannot be seen as an expression of God's love.

Ian Barbour has declared that the idea of the creation of the world out of nothing (*ex nihilo*) is not a biblical concept. He shares the view of many philosophers and theologians who consider that the concept developed as a defence against the ideas of the religious movement known as Gnosticism. Gnostics believe that the pre-existing matter from which the universe was created was evil or the product of an inferior god. Central to Gnosticism is the belief that humans are divine souls trapped in a world created by an imperfect spirit or god (the demiurge). Some Gnostics believe that the demiurge is an embodiment of evil whereas other Gnostics consider the spirit to be benevolent but imperfect, and therefore limited. Alongside the demiurge there exists a supreme being who is unknowable, remote but the embodiment of all that is good. Humans can only be freed from the inferior material world through spiritual knowledge of their true origins, their essential nature and their ultimate destiny. This knowledge is only available to all through direct experience or knowledge (gnosis) of God. For Christian Gnostics this knowledge was brought by Jesus.

Link

Look back at p80 and remind yourself of Alvin Plantinga's critique of Mackie, which is given as the second strength of Augustine's theodicy.

Activity

What do you think?

Organise a class debate to consider whether or not free will is a satisfactory explanation for the existence of evil in a world created by God.

AQA Examiner's tip

The issues you will be exploring are complex, so do not expect all assessment questions to have straightforward black and white, yes or no answers. The views or claims you are given to assess may have strong arguments both in their support and against them, but these arguments will also have weaknesses, so make sure that you follow them through.

Link

Look back to p68 and remind yourself of the meaning of Gnosticism and its influence on St Augustine's theodicy.

Think about

As a theodicy is seeking to justify the God of classical theism in the face of the apparent existence of evil, why do you think that many scholars prefer the term 'process thought' rather than 'process theodicy' for this philosophy?

Take it further

Find out more about the religious world view of A. N. Whitehead.

Process thought

Process philosophy is a distinctive religious world view based upon the work of A. N. Whitehead (1861–1947). David Griffin developed a theodicy on the basis of process philosophy in his book *God, Power and Evil: A Process Theodicy*. It seeks to respond to the challenge that the amount of suffering in the world is too great and often unjust to be explained by the suggestion that it is for the development of human virtues.

Many scholars will not accept that this is a theodicy and prefer to call it process thought. This is because unlike the other arguments considered so far, process thought accepts David Hume's view that evil is incompatible with the existence of an omnipotent, all-loving God, and it starts from the assumption that God is not omnipotent but God is good. As God is no longer regarded in this philosophy as all-powerful then God can no longer have created the world out of nothing.

God's role in creation

Process theologians do not use the usual translation of Genesis 1:1, 'In the beginning, God created the heavens and the earth', but the other translation of some Hebrew scholars, 'When God began to create the heavens and the earth, the earth was without form and void'. Griffin argues that this translation supports the universe as uncreated and eternal, and having within it the deity. As God is not the creator of the natural laws then God is limited by these laws, and is therefore not omnipotent.

If this view is accepted then God's role in creation was limited to developing what was already there, for example by encouraging the start of the evolutionary process. In every situation, God works by 'persuading' and 'luring' creation towards a state of greater order and complexity, in which the two kinds of goodness are to be found: harmony and intensity. Where creation rebels against God's persuasion, for He does not have the power to impose His will, the corresponding evils of discord (including physical and mental pain) and pointless triviality will result.

As the creative process develops, the possibilities for good and evil both increase, as both harmony and discord can be experienced in greater intensity. With the development of humans who exert their own influence on the world, God's control is further diminished, since humans are free to ignore God. Their knowledge of God's will is very limited since He did not fashion them after His own likeness. Hence Griffin believes that it is necessarily the case that God cannot completely control the creatures:

> God cannot coerce worldly beings, because the inherent power they have cannot be overridden.

David Griffin, Process Theodicy, Christology, and the Imitatio Dei, *1996*

By admitting the limits to God's power, process theodicy no longer needs to justify why God does not intervene to stop evil, for God is simply unable to do this. However, this does not free God from responsibility for evil altogether. It was, after all, God who started off the process of ordering the universe, knowing that He would be unable to control it. In Griffin's words:

> God is responsible for evil in the sense of having urged the creation forward to those states in which discordant feelings could be felt with greater intensity.

David Griffin, God, Power and Evil: A Process Theodicy, *1976*

The main task of the process theodicy therefore is to explain satisfactorily why God took such a risk rather than allowing the original matter to remain chaotic and undisturbed. Griffin argues that the:

> question as to whether God is indictable is to be answered in terms of the question as to whether the positive values that are possible in our world are valuable enough to be worth the risk of the negative experiences which have occurred, and the even greater horrors which stand before us as real possibilities for the future. Should God, for the sake of avoiding the possibility of persons such as Hitler, and horrors such as Auschwitz, have precluded the possibility of Jesus, Gautama, Socrates, Confucius, Moses, Mendelssohn, El Greco, Michelangelo, Leonardo da Vinci ... and millions of other marvellous human beings, well known and not well known alike, who have lived on the face of this earth? In other words, should God, for the sake of avoiding 'man's inhumanity to man,' have avoided humanity (or some comparably complex species) altogether? Only those who could sincerely answer this question affirmatively could indict the God of process theology on the basis of the evil in the world.

David Griffin, God, Power and Evil: A Process Theodicy, *1976*

Griffin is arguing here that God can only be condemned for setting off the creative process if we genuinely believe that, in order to avoid the risk of evil, He should also have avoided all possibilities of good. Griffin suggests that the universe has produced enough quantity and quality of good to outweigh the evil, so that given a choice between the universe we live in and no universe at all, the former is preferable. This, it is argued, justifies God's choice.

God suffers as well

An important feature of process theodicy is that God Himself suffers along with the world every time His creative desires are frustrated, such as when moral evil is committed. This follows naturally from the fact that God is part of the world, affected by it, yet unable to control it. For Whitehead, God is not a last resort transcendent from the world and remaining independent of it. Instead, God is an integral element in the world and participates actively in its struggles and concerns. The outcome is as Whitehead states in *Process and Reality*, that God is the 'fellow sufferer who understands'. This makes it much easier to justify God in the face of the risk that He took. For, as Griffin writes, it:

> not only removes the basis for that sense of moral outrage which would be directed toward an impassive spectator deity who took great risks with the creation. It also provides an additional basis, beyond that of our own immediate experience, for affirming that the risk was worth taking. That being who is the universal agent, goading the creation to overcome triviality in favour of the more intense harmonies, is also the universal recipient of the totality of good and evil that is actualized. In other words, the one being who is in a position to know experientially the bitter as well as the sweet fruits of the risk of creation is the same being who has encouraged and continues to encourage this process of creative risk taking.

David Griffin, God, Power and Evil: A Process Theodicy, *1976*

Think about

According to Griffin, what is God's role in creation?

Take it further

Using the internet and/or library find out more about what Griffin and Whitehead believe is the purpose of evil.

It would therefore be unreasonable for humans to condemn God for His role in the creative process when He has suffered unimaginably more than anyone else from the consequences, having experienced every suffering that there has ever been. Likewise, it would be unreasonable for anyone else to suggest that they know better than God whether the whole process has been and continues to be worthwhile. If it is good enough for God, so to speak, then it should be good enough for everyone else.

The purpose of evil in process thought

In the theodicies we have studied, theologians are arguing in effect that there is no genuine evil because all the evil is merely apparent evil since it contributes to a greater good, as it is by overcoming evil that people can become closer to God. In process thought evil is required, for the:

> correlation between the capacity to enjoy and the capacity to suffer is a necessary, metaphysical correlation, inherent in the nature of things.
>
> *David Griffin*, Creation Out of Chaos and the Problem of Evil, *1981*

In process thought evil is regarded as discord in the world that brings about destruction. In *Adventures of Ideas*, Whitehead describes evil as 'in itself destructive and evil' and concludes that 'destruction as a dominant fact in the experience is the correct definition of evil'. But from this discord there can be benefits. It allows for the recognition of perfection and generates the desire for a better world.

In other words we cannot experience all of the values if we have not opposites. If, for example, we are going to experience enjoyment, happiness, goodness then the opposites must exist of misery, sadness and evil. Situations with which we are presented have the choice of acting for good or evil. Griffin believes that suffering is part of life and can only be avoided by bringing humanity to an end by not reproducing.

> If the moral aim could be adequately expressed as the intention to avoid suffering, then moral adults would never have children—that would be the way to guarantee that they would never have children who would suffer or cause suffering.
>
> *David Griffin*, Creation Out of Chaos and the Problem of Evil, *1981*

Evil in process thought is not just actions that bring about suffering, but also opportunities missed to bring about good.

> In other words, suffering and sinful intentions resulting in suffering are not the only forms of evil. Any absence of good that could have been realized is evil even if no suffering is involved. Recall that the definition of genuine evil offered earlier was 'anything which makes the world worse than it could have otherwise been.' Any absence of good that makes the world worse than it could have been, all things considered, is an evil. Hence, for God to have failed to bring forth beings capable of experiencing significant value when this was possible would have made God indictable.
>
> *David Griffin*, Creation Out of Chaos and the Problem of Evil, *1981*

Griffin cannot support the view that moral evil is so great that it would be better for a world in which such lives are lived never to have existed.

Natural evil is explained by the suggestion that all creatures can deviate from God's will and this caused natural evil. As God is not working with materials that were in a perfect state when He created the world then there is scope for natural disasters when these materials fail.

The strengths of process thought

To its followers, process thought has a number of advantages:

- It removes the stumbling block of why, if God is all-loving and omnipotent, He does not put an end to all suffering. It removes it with the simple answer that He cannot. The process theodicy is therefore the only one to avoid the troublesome thought that if God really wanted to He could make it all better. Despite the attempts to explain that God has good reason not to, none of these is without its problems, leading many to suspect that God is not really all-loving. Process theodicy avoids this suspicion.

- For religious believers, the fact that God suffers may be encouraging, since people realise that God can have personal experience of what they are going through. It can be argued that a deeper, more loving and trusting relationship is possible with a God who truly suffers alongside people than with a God who is safely cocooned from the effects of evil.

- Since the process God suffers from all of the evils that have ever afflicted the world, and yet continues to draw the creative process on, the believer can be reassured that his or her own struggle is worth the strife.

- Within the process scheme, there is no certainty that God will triumph in the end. The theodicy may therefore encourage some believers to join in the fight against evil and secure victory. It is not a theodicy which encourages inertia, for this would result in disaster for all.

The weakness of process thought

Despite the strengths of process thought there have been severe criticisms. These include the rejection by many of its adherents that it is a theodicy. It is thought to be a major weakness that process thought is not a justification of God in the face of evil. Since process philosophy removes the concept of omnipotence from God, it does not in fact justify Him at all. It in fact denies the God of classical theism. The process approach is therefore unacceptable to many on both religious and philosophical grounds. For example, it can be argued that omnipotence is such a crucial attribute of God that a being with such limited power as the process 'God' would not be worthy of worship.

A major strength of process thought is supposed to be its view of God as the 'fellow sufferer who understands'. But there is no *need* to accept process thought to see him in this way, and there is good reason not to, as it leads only to despair. In traditional Christian thought, God experiences the pain and suffering of crucifixion through becoming incarnate in Jesus. But here the crucial difference is that God *chooses* to allow this experience, maintains His omnipotence and offers the certainty that in the future, wrongs will be righted and good will triumph. There is a world of difference between a God who understands from His position of strength and a God who understands merely because, in the words of Brian Davis, He is 'in the soup' as well (*The Reality of God and the Problem of Evil*, 2006). Since He offers no solution to our helplessness, the process God again seems not to be worthy of worship.

Think about

What do you think are the main strengths and weaknesses of the process theodicy? Overall, do you consider it more or less successful than the other theodicies in this chapter?

Activity

Write a 500–600-word essay explaining how process thought seeks to overcome the problem of evil.

Think about

- Imagine you are about to play a football match. It is an important event and you have prepared well. You know that your opponents are good players.
- How would this affect your attitude and the way you would play?

Activities

1. List the reasons why you would not be willing to worship a God with limited power.

2. If your life were to contain a lot of suffering, how much of a comfort would it be that your limited God was suffering alongside you?

Think about

Look back at Ivan Karamazov's reasons for rejecting God on p88. How similar is his view to that of Brian Davies?

While for some the uncertainty of the future could encourage a valiant effort, for others it may simply fill them with desperation. If God cannot guarantee anything, what is the point of human efforts? The very fact that they may all come to nothing would be enough to put many off trying in the first place.

Finally, the theodicy has justified God's initiating evolution on the grounds that good has outweighed evil. But it is unlikely that this justification would appeal to those who have only undergone the suffering. Since there is no promise of Heaven, there is no certainty that the suffering of the innocent will ever be compensated. The fact that nature has produced a Leonardo da Vinci hardly makes up for the suffering and deaths of those involved in the Indian Ocean tsunami! In the words of Barbara Ward and René Dubos:

> The actual life of most of mankind has been cramped with back-breaking labour, exposed to deadly or debilitating diseases, prey to wars and famines, haunted by the loss of children, filled with fear and the ignorance that breeds more fear. At the end, for everyone, stands dreaded unknown death.

B. Ward and R. Dubos, Only One Earth: The Care and Maintenance of a Small Planet, *1972*

> ### Think about
>
> What do you think Barbara Ward and René Dubos are saying about human suffering in the quote from *Only One Earth*?

Even if it were true that God has experienced more pain than anyone else (and it could be impossible to compare the 'feelings' of a divine being spread throughout creation with those of a human focused in one small part), it must be the case that He has also reaped more joy than anyone else. From God's point of view, then, the benefits may well outweigh the suffering, and there is the ever-present appeal of future harmonies of even greater intensity. But for the people described by Ward and Dubos, who have only known the pain, have never known the joys and may never know them as they are now dead with no guarantee of an afterlife, there is no such justification. Taking their perspective into account, God can easily be condemned or 'indicted' for urging the process on.

> ### Think about
>
> - Which do you think poses the greatest challenge to faith in God – natural evil or moral evil?
> - Give reasons for your view.

💡 Is natural or moral evil the greater challenge to faith?

The answer that the majority of believers and philosophers would give to this question is natural evil. Moral evil can be explained by humans choosing to act against God's laws and giving in to temptation, and it is therefore under human control. Many philosophers have argued that moral evil is the unavoidable risk that free will entails. Natural evil on the other hand is beyond human control and is unpredictable. The vast suffering caused by an earthquake, famine or tsunami seems to be without purpose, especially as it frequently seems that the innocent suffer. This is used by many atheists to reject the belief in an omnipotent, all-loving God. John Stuart Mill argued that the existence of suffering and pain in the natural world was a reason for rejecting God.

> ### Link
>
> Look back at p84. What did Hick mean by the counterfactual hypothesis?

However, the result of this difficulty is that many reasons have been developed to explain natural evil. Augustine blames such evil on the disruption to the harmony of God's creation caused by the fallen angels and Adam and Eve, whereas Hick's counterfactual hypothesis suggests that such evil is necessary as part of the means by which humanity is able to develop into the likeness of God. And process theodicy has no greater difficulty accounting for natural than moral evil, by tracing both of them back to the inherent chaos within uncreated matter.

It is true that in modern society many do not accept the existence of the Devil and fallen angels, and therefore find such an explanation for natural evil difficult to accept. However, there are many who would accept to some extent that natural evil is the result of the imbalance in the harmony of God's creation caused by humanity. Famine, for example, is often the result of human greed, and many natural disasters could be the result of a lack of concern in the past for the environment.

Not all philosophers would consider natural evil a greater problem than moral evil. We have seen how process thought explains them both in the same way. From a different perspective, D. Z. Phillips' criticism that suffering cannot be justified by love would make moral and natural evils equally problematic. Some could even argue that moral evil is a greater problem than natural. In Augustine's theodicy, natural evil is easily accounted for as a punishment, whereas it may be harder to explain why the initial act of moral evil ever happened. And Mackie's argument that God could have created free beings who would never choose to sin suggests moral evil is totally unnecessary, whereas some natural evil could perhaps be seen as a challenge to aid human development.

Take it further

Using the internet find out more about the different understandings of the concept of the Devil and fallen angels.

Think about

- Each of the religious responses to the problem of evil has tried to provide adequate explanations for both moral and natural evil so that it is possible to keep faith in God.
- Which of these responses do you think have achieved their aim most successfully?

Activities

1 Read the story of Job in the book of Job in the Old Testament.

2 Write an account of Job's suffering and the reasons given for his suffering.

3 What was Job's understanding of the cause of his suffering by the end of the story?

Conclusion

There is no universally accepted solution to the problem of evil. There are many examples of suffering that appear to have no purpose since they lead only to destruction and death. For those who already feel that the existence of God is improbable, the problem of evil will merely strengthen this conviction.

However, believers in the God of classical theism must implicitly have found a solution that they find acceptable. Some may concentrate upon the evidence for God's goodness to humanity, as demonstrated in gifts such as eternal life. Some appeal to the view that since we are only human, we cannot understand the ways of the divine, and that God, in His infinite wisdom and purpose, must have some deep and unavoidable purpose for the existence of evil. This view is not illogical because it is not logically impossible that the God of classical theism might have some use for evil within His creation that is beyond human understanding and therefore from a human perspective makes some suffering appear pointless. In Hick's words:

> Our 'solution', then, to this baffling problem of excessive and undeserved suffering is a frank appeal to the positive power of mystery. Such suffering remains unjust and inexplicable, haphazard and cruelly excessive. The mystery of dysteleological suffering is a real mystery, impenetrable to the rationalizing human mind.

John Hick, Evil and the God of Love, *1978*

Think about

We all accept that certain things, such as the law of gravity, exist, even if we are unable to explain them fully. Is it any more unreasonable, therefore, to accept the existence of God, even though we cannot explain suffering?

■ Further reading and weblinks

Davies, B. *An Introduction to the Philosophy of Religion* (3rd edn), Oxford University Press, 1993. Chapter 10 contains an interesting and readable discussion of the problem of evil.

Griffin, D. R. *God, Power and Evil: A Process Theodicy*, The Westminster Press, 1976. The book focuses on process thought (theodicy).

Hick, J. *Evil and the God of Love* (2nd edn), Harper, 1985. This contains excellent accounts of not only Hick's soul-making theodicy but also several theodicies in the Augustinian tradition, as well as several criticisms and an account of the problem of evil.

Hick, J. H. *Philosophy of Religion*, Prentice Hall, 1990. Chapter 4 contains useful summaries of all the required theodicies including process thought.

Medieval Sourcebook: Augustine (354–430): *The City of God*, www.fordham.edu/halsall/source/aug-city2.html. This site has extracts from Augustine's, *The City of God*.

Taliaferro, C. and Griffiths, P. J. *Philosophy of Religion, An Anthology*, Wiley-Blackwell, 2003. This book contains William Rowe's essay 'The Problem of Evil and Some Varieties of Atheism' that considers the evidential problem of evil.

The Nature of Evil and the Irenaean Theodicy, www.revneal.org/Writings/evil.htm. Rev. Gregory S. Neal examines the nature of evil and the Irenaean theodicy.

Vardy, P. and Arliss, J. *The Thinker's Guide to Evil*, John Hunt Publishing, 2003. This book is a good explanation of the problem of evil at a level appropriate to all A2 Level students.

Now that you have completed this chapter, you should be able to:

- explain the concept of evil (natural and moral)

- analyse the logical and evidential problem of evil

- summarise religious responses to the problem of evil, including theodicies in the Augustinian tradition, the free-will defence, John Hick's 'vale of soul-making' theodicy and process thought

- evaluate the success of the theodicies as a response to the problem of evil, including their strengths and weaknesses

- evaluate whether free will is a satisfactory explanation for the existence of evil in a world created by God

- evaluate what poses the greatest challenge to faith in God – natural or moral evil

- evaluate whether free will is a satisfactory explanation for the existence of evil in a world created by God.

Summary of key points

■ Chapter 1: The ontological argument and the relationship between reason and faith

Anselm

- *Proslogion 2* – 'God is that than which nothing greater can be conceived.' Even the unbeliever must have a definition of God in order to dismiss it as a concept.
- If this definition is accepted, God must exist in reality, 'as that which exists in reality will always be greater than that which exists purely in intellect' (or in the mind/understanding).
- *Proslogion 3* – it is possible to conceive of a being whose existence is necessary.
- God must be such a being if He is 'that than which nothing greater can be conceived'. This is because a being that possesses necessary existence will always be greater than a contingent being.

Descartes

- 'God is a supremely perfect being.'
- 'Existence' is a perfection.
- To think of God without existence, therefore, is like thinking of a triangle without its three sides.
- It is therefore illogical to consider the concept of God without the concept of existence.

These arguments are examples of *reductio ad absurdum* arguments; they begin with a proposition, and attempt to prove (through logical reasoning) that it would be 'absurd' to reject the proposition.

How successful are these arguments?

Gaunilo

- 'The most perfect island' can be understood, but that does not mean it exists.
- Whilst Anselm never compares two things of a like kind, Gaunilo is occupied with comparisons of similarities (that is, islands).
- This criticism of Anselm does not work as it assumes that it is coherent to conceive of an island than which none more perfect can be conceived; it is not coherent.
- As Plantinga suggests, islands have no intrinsic maximum; that is, they can always be bettered.

David Hume

- Hume suggested that it was impossible to start with a concept in the mind (that is, a definition), apply pure logic and reach an external, objective conclusion (that is, 'God exists').
- He also claimed, like others, that existence cannot be treated as a predicate which 'adds something' to the definition of a subject.

Gottlob Frege

■ Existence is a 'second-order predicate'.

■ Frege distinguishes between first- and second-order predicates. He suggests that first-order predicates tell us something about the subject, whereas second-order predicates tell us about concepts.

■ It would seem that Anselm is regarding existence as a first-order predicate, which it cannot be as it tells us nothing about the subject.

Immanuel Kant

Kant has two basic objections:

■ Firstly, that there is no contradiction in dismissing both a subject and its associated predicate (that is, God and existence). This successfully challenges Descartes.

■ Secondly, that 'existence is not a predicate'. If it were, it would be something that a thing either had or lacked (like blue eyes). However, this creates a paradox in saying that something does not exist; how could such a thing lack (or indeed possess) anything?

Bertrand Russell

Russell claims that Anselm uses the word 'exist' incorrectly. Existence cannot be a predicate.

Norman Malcolm

■ If God is 'that than which nothing greater can be conceived', He cannot be brought into existence, nor can He simply happen to come into existence (as this would require the input of a greater being and would render God limited and finite).

■ Therefore, God's existence is either necessary (if He does exist), or impossible (if He does not).

■ Unless God's necessary existence presents us with a logical contradiction, we must accept it.

Criticisms

■ Malcolm argues that stating that God possesses necessary existence, means that we can conclude logically and acceptably that God must exist. Brian Davies challenges this; he believes that Malcolm has failed to recognise that the word 'is' can be used in different ways.

■ On the one hand it can be used to describe something ('the horse is brown'), and on the other it can be used to explain that there actually is something ('there is such a thing as a dragon'). Whilst the first use is clearly descriptive, Davies argues that the second use tells us nothing, yet leaves the listener having to suppose the existence of the subject. However, this is unacceptable, as we could literally define anything into existence!

Alvin Plantinga

■ 'Possible worlds'.

■ There is a possible world in which there is a being with 'maximal greatness'.

■ A being only has 'maximal greatness' if it exists in every world. Therefore, such a being exists in our world.

■ However, this does not mean God.

■ A problem exists; even if the being exists in every world, there could exist in each separate world an individual being that is greater.

■ Therefore, Plantinga suggests 'maximal excellence'.

■ If we apply this and 'maximal greatness' to the being, we can conclude that there is a God whose existence follows from His essence.

Criticisms

■ Some would dismiss Plantinga by attacking the whole concept of 'possible worlds'.

■ However, criticism can also focus upon his assumption that claiming there is a being with 'maximal excellence' in every world, means that such a being must exist in our world. This is not the case. All that follows is that 'maximal excellence' is possible, and therefore God is possible, not actual.

The significance of the ontological argument for faith

■ The debate is whether or not the ontological argument goes beyond defining God and helps to strengthen faith or even to convince people of the existence of God.

■ Gaunilo and Russell both argue that it possibly helps people to understand the concept of the God of classical theism, but that does not mean that it will change an atheist's view that God does not exist.

■ As Kant points out, it is possible to have a definition of God as it is also possible to have a definition of a triangle, but the triangle can be rejected altogether as can 'the concept of an absolutely necessary being'.

■ It may be that the argument is more successful to help the believer develop a greater understanding of the attributes of God.

■ Chapter 2: Religious language

How do you speak about God?

For some philosophers it is by talking about what God is not – the *via negativa*. Make sure you know the teaching about the *via negativa* of:

■ St John of the Cross

■ Dionysius the Pseudo-Areopagite and the apophatic way.

Meaningfulness of religious language

Verification principle

A statement is only meaningful (logical) if we know how it can be proved true or false; either because it is an analytical statement or through empirical methods.

■ Logical positivists (Vienna Circle) considered religious language meaningless because it could not be tested empirically and was not analytic.

■ A. J. Ayer developed the strong and weak versions of the argument.

Responses to the verification principle

Falsification principle

A statement is only meaningful if we accept that evidence may count against it. Religious language is considered meaningless because believers will not allow anything to count against their beliefs.

Antony Flew argued that religious language dies the 'death of a thousand qualifications' because believers do not allow anything to count against their beliefs, and keep qualifying beliefs when anything appears to count against them. Flew used John Wisdom's *Parable of the Gardener* to demonstrate how believers and unbelievers express different reactions to the same 'facts'.

Criticisms

- John Hick criticised the principle on the grounds of eschatological verification.
- R. M. Hare's 'bliks'.
- Basil Mitchell – a believer is expected to have faith, even when the evidence appears to go against the beliefs.
- Richard Swinburne – things have meaning even if we know we can never prove them true or false. He used the example of the toys in the toy cupboard.

Religious language does have a purpose

R. B. Braithwaite said that religious language does not convey facts, but is a means of expressing emotion and morality (non-cognitive).

Religious language as analogy

Religious language consists of *analogies* that allow people to talk about God and faith:

- St Thomas Aquinas – analogies of proportion and analogies of attribution.
- Ian Ramsey – models/qualifiers.

Religious language is symbolic

- Paul Tillich – symbols point us to 'being itself'.
- J. R. Randall – religious language is not factual but takes us beyond facts to the *ultimate* reality.
- Carl Jung's belief that the archetypes of human experience reveal themselves in the universal symbols of art and religion.

Religious truths are conveyed through myths

- Aetiological myths provide foundation ideas for religious approaches.
- Rudolph Bultman argued that the truth of Christianity is to be discovered in the mythological language of the New Testament.

Religious language is a language game

Ludwig Wittgenstein stated that each human activity has its own language 'game'. If you are not in the 'game', you will not understand the language and the result is that it will appear meaningless to you. Therefore if you are not a believer, any talk about God and faith will be meaningless and appear to have no purpose.

Chapter 3: Body, soul and personal identity

Resurrection is the belief found in Christianity, Islam and Judaism that from the moment of birth each person has an immortal soul that survives death. (This sounds like disembodied existence!) The question philosophers ask is whether that soul survives within a physical or spiritual form, and when this resurrection occurs.

A distinction is often drawn between the *body* and the *soul* of a human being. The body is normally seen as a physical object that lives, dies and then decomposes. The soul is generally associated with an individual's personality, decisions and free will, and is often linked to the mind; sometimes the two terms are used interchangeably. However, the identity and even existence of the soul are open to intense debate. The soul is often understood to be immaterial and spiritual, rather than physical. This would enable it to survive independently after the death of the body, making it immortal in its own right. It would also raise the question of how such a soul might be considered to interact with the physical body. An alternative approach identifies the soul more closely with the physical body, suggesting that the soul could only survive the death of the body if the body itself were resurrected. However, there is a wide range of variations upon these two approaches, meaning that they are not always easy to distinguish. Some, of course, consider that the soul does not exist at all, at least in any objective sense. According to this view, 'soul' is merely a word that some people use to describe their *experience* of personal identity. Some would consider even this experience to be an illusion.

Key materialists

Materialists argue that there is no such thing as an immaterial soul that is separate from the physical body.

■ Gilbert Ryle in *The Concept of the Mind* (1949) argued that we make a category mistake by thinking that the noun 'soul' refers to a concrete object in the way that the noun 'body' does. It is like a foreigner watching a cricket match asking which is the 'team spirit'. It is a mistake leading people to imagine there is a 'soul' like a 'ghost in the machine'. Ryle opposed the dualist separation between a tangible body and an intangible mind or soul. All references to the mental must be understood in terms of witnessable activities. We can see that the physical affects the mental and vice versa.

■ Richard Dawkins supports materialism and rejects dualism because he argues that we are no more than DNA carriers – 'just bytes and bytes of digital information' (*River out of Eden*, 1995). Belief in an immortal soul is outdated and there is no scientific evidence to support it. Evolution is the only rational theory and it is our genetic make-up that guides us. The genes are found in behaviour (does this mean they *influence* our behaviour?), so our bodies acquire individuality. We feel like single organisms, not a colony, as selection has favoured genes that cooperate. It is our genes working together that give us a sense of individuality, not the soul. The colony needs a central control. The genetic model becomes more complex and thinks about itself as an individual and considers the consequences of its actions. 'Consciousness arises when the brain's simulation of the world becomes so complete that it must include a model of itself' (*The Selfish Gene*, 1976). This leads to human culture, a 'replicator' or 'memes' (tunes, catchphrases, quotes, teachings), which are heard and lodge in the brain, and are then imitated by it. At death we leave behind genes and memes, though the genes will quickly be dispersed. The need for DNA survival brings about the belief in an individual consciousness which is mistakenly thought of as an immortal soul. It is this belief that creates culture.

Key dualists

Dualists argue that the body and soul are two separate things and accept the immortality of the soul; whereas the body decays, the soul continues after death.

■ Plato was a dualist. He believed that the soul and the body are two separate substances that interact. Plato stated that the soul belonged to a higher level of reality than the body. He thought that the soul is a (non-physical?) substance and is immortal. The physical body hinders the soul since the needs of the physical such as hunger and thirst intrude on the efforts made by the soul to contemplate the Forms. The function of the mind is to control the two. (Plato compares the mind to a charioteer trying to control two horses that seek to go in different directions.) If the physical desires can be overcome then the soul can acquire knowledge of the Reality and after death break from the cycle of birth and death and remain in the realm of the Forms.

■ Descartes argued that the body and mind (soul) are different substances. The soul survives death but the body decays. Descartes argued that while we can doubt material existence, we cannot doubt our own existence – 'I think therefore I am'. Even if we are dreaming or under the control of a demon, we still have our own thoughts. Therefore the physical and non-physical are distinct substances with distinct properties. The physical self takes up space but the soul is of a different substance that does not need to take up space.

Materialists who accept life after death would argue that survival after death would have to include the resurrection of the body. Since, after death, our physical bodies decay, we would have to receive a replica body, and this is the basis of John Hick's replica theory. Aristotle's theory is like, but is not, materialism. Aristotle did not believe in an afterlife or the immortality of the soul. He considered the 'soul' to be the part of the body which gave it life.

John Hick's replica theory

The replica theory is based on the idea that if someone dies and then appears in a new place, it is meaningful to call this replica the same person. In the same way, when a person dies, a replica of that person appears in the afterlife. The replica theory supports materialism because it assumes that life after death would require a replica of the 'whole' person including the physical self.

Hick said that God is all-powerful and could create a replica body complete with memories and characteristics in the next life and this replica is the same person. However, the very fact that it is a replica means that it is not the original. In the same way if an exact copy of the *Mona Lisa* is made, people would not regard it as the original.

Other problems include the fact that if God can make one replica, He could make multiple replicas; which then is the same person as the original? Hick assumes it is reasonable to conceive a place inhabited by resurrected persons, although this is entirely outside our experience. If the replicas have physical bodies then they are going to be affected by the same restrictions on movement and need for space that we have in this world. It also raises the question of whether it would suffer from the same physical defects as the original. St Paul, by contrast, described the resurrected body as a spiritual body, though it may be hard to see how a body without physical form could be a body at all.

Reincarnation and rebirth are the beliefs found in Hinduism and Buddhism. Reincarnation accepts the transmigration of souls. At death, the soul leaves the body that it currently inhabits and eventually starts another life in another physical body. Rebirth is a similar concept, except that the continuity between the person who died and the person who is reborn is considered to be less strong. However, in both cases, each new life is influenced by the karma from the previous lives. The ultimate aim is to achieve perfection so that there is no further need to be reborn and a state of bliss is achieved.

Evidence to support life after death

- Regression to past lives – or, is the person remembering past lives or remembering experiences and knowledge gained earlier in this life?
- 'Sightings of dead people' – or, are these sightings of the spirits of the dead, hallucinations or a 'tape' of past events?
- Spiritualism – or, are mediums contacting the dead, or are they thought-readers of the living?

Near-death experiences

A near-death experience comprises memories of events that were experienced by the patient in the short space of time during which they were declared clinically dead.

Reasons for accepting NDEs as evidence for life after death include:

- clear recollection of all that happened during the experience
- life-changing nature – many become more interested in spiritual rather than material things, even changing their way of life
- conviction that there is life after death and there is nothing to fear
- belief that they have learnt that the most important thing in life is love of others
- they are experienced by children who describe things they could not understand – work of Dr Melvin Morse
- detail given while 'dead' of things happening around them – especially Pam Reynolds
- found in all parts of the world and affect people regardless of race, creed, sex or age – work of Dr Raymond Moody.

Reasons for rejecting NDEs as evidence for life after death include:

- temporal lobe epilepsy
- hypoxia
- effect of the illness
- not really dead
- there can be no life after death – humans are just DNA carriers
- US jet pilots have similar experiences under the influence of G force.

■ Chapter 4: The problem of evil

Moral evil is caused by human beings, whereas *natural* evil exists independently of human actions.

Both types of evil result in the *suffering* of innocent people.

The problem of evil

For religious people, the existence of suffering and evil poses a challenge to belief in the God of classical theism.

The *logical* problem of evil is the view that evil makes God's existence *impossible*:

■ It is logically inconsistent to accept both the existence of evil and of God. An all-knowing and all-powerful God would be able to prevent evil and suffering. An all-loving God would want to prevent evil and suffering. That God does not calls into question his omnipotence, omnibenevolence or existence. David Hume took this view.

■ It also makes it *impossible* for those whose definition of God includes the concept of *infinite goodness*, where God's goodness is understood to equal our definition of the term. Upholders of this point of view argue that the existence of *any* evil removes the infinity of God's goodness. Aquinas considered this point of view.

The *evidential* problem of evil is the view that although it is not logically inconsistent to accept both evil and God, since it is logically possible that God could have a good reason for allowing evil, evil nevertheless makes his existence *improbable*.

■ The existence of evil counts as evidence against the likelihood of an all-loving and all-powerful God, for evil *most likely* suggests that God is limited in power, or is not all-loving, or that He does not exist.

■ William Rowe's version of the evidential problem of evil focuses on examples of *pointless* human and animal suffering. These examples point towards atheism because, at worst, a loving God would only allow evil that was essential for a 'greater good'.

A theodicy is an attempt to justify God in the face of evil.

Augustine's theodicy

The main themes of theodicies in the Augustinian tradition are as follows:

■ God is omnipotent and all-loving.

■ God created a perfect world.

■ Angels and humans brought *moral* evil into the world through the abuse of free will.

■ *Natural evil* results from the breakdown of the natural order following moral evil.

■ Evil is an *absence of good*, not a substance, so God cannot have created it.

■ Everyone was present in Adam, so everyone deserves to suffer as a punishment.

■ God's mercy means that some will be saved and go to Heaven.

- Augustine's aesthetic argument states that evil only exists when parts of the world are considered in isolation from the whole. When the entirety of creation is considered, it is wholly good.

The main themes of Augustine's theodicy have been adapted and developed by many others including Aquinas, Leibniz and Calvin. The free-will defence is also a development of one of the key themes used by Augustine.

Criticisms

- Evil cannot create itself out of perfection.

- It is *not* fair for us to suffer since we were not all in Adam.

- Likewise, science tells us that humans were *never* created in perfection.

- The fact that God created the world despite knowing that the Fall would happen suggests that evil and the punishment of Hell were part of God's plan. He is unfair to send some to Heaven. Calvin's view of predestination is especially criticised.

The free-will defence

- This develops the emphasis of the Augustinian and Irenaean theodicies upon free will. Proponents include Richard Swinburne and Alvin Plantinga.

- The main debate centres on whether God could have created free beings which would always choose to obey Him. Mackie argues that He could.

- If so, the free-will defence fails, along with the classical theodicies.

- Hick and Plantinga argue that free beings cannot be guaranteed to always choose good.

John Hick's vale of soul-making theodicy

- God is omnipotent and all-loving.

- He did *not* make a perfect world because true goodness has to be developed rather than being ready made.

- True goodness requires free will which justifies the potential for evil.

- Actual evil (moral *and* natural) is justified by its power to enable us to develop. The world was made as a place of 'soul-making', not as a paradise.

- Everyone will be rewarded in Heaven.

Criticisms

- The idea that everyone will go to Heaven is unfair and removes the point of obeying God.

- The theodicy does not explain why suffering should be so *excessive*. Nor does it explain *pointless* evil, which benefits no one.

- D. Z. Phillips argues that an all-loving God would not make people suffer for any purpose.

The strengths and weaknesses of the Augustinian theodicies, Hick's theodicy and the various formulations of the free-will defence offer a variety of opinions as to the extent to which free will is a satisfactory explanation for the existence of evil in a world created by God.

Process thought

This was developed by David Griffin.

■ God is loving but not omnipotent.

■ God's role in creation was limited to setting off the evolution process.

■ God cannot prevent moral or natural evil since the world and its creatures are beyond His control.

■ God was justified in encouraging evolution because the good results have outweighed the evil.

■ God suffers along with His creation.

Criticisms

■ It is not a *theodicy* since it offers no defence of the God of classical theism.

■ God was not justified in his decision to start evolution when He could not control the process. It is unfair that some prosper whilst others suffer.

■ It is unjustifiable simply to 'come up' with a new definition of God to try to explain evil and suffering.

The different theodicies offer a variety of views as to whether moral or natural evil poses the greater threat to belief in God. Natural evil is often considered the greater problem as it can be accounted for less easily in relation to human free will unless it is seen as a punishment as in the Augustinian tradition. However, arguments such as Hick's counterfactual hypothesis have gone some way to answering this challenge.

AQA Examination-style questions

AQA Examiner's tip

You only have 45 minutes to answer a question! Try to allocate your time according to the number of marks available. Twenty-seven minutes including thinking time for part (a) and 18 minutes for part (b). *Do not rush* – and take care with your handwriting. Time spent planning your answer is time well spent, and there is no point in writing something the examiner cannot read.

1   (a)   Explain the traditional forms of the ontological argument as put forward by Anselm and Descartes.   *(30 marks)*

       (b)   'The ontological argument is only in the mind and is therefore a weak argument.' Discuss.   *(20 marks)*

2   (a)   Explain why it is difficult to talk meaningfully about God.   *(30 marks)*

       (b)   Assess the claim that the purpose of religious language is not to describe God but to evoke a sense of His presence.   *(20 marks)*

3   (a)   Explain how different philosophers have understood the idea that people have souls.   *(30 marks)*

       (b)   'All concepts of life after death are just wishful thinking.' Discuss.   *(20 marks)*

4   (a)   Explain how process thought seeks to provide a religious response to the problem of evil.   *(30 marks)*

       (b)   Evaluate the claim that the existence of natural evil in the world makes it impossible to believe in a God who is all-loving and all-powerful.   *(20 marks)*

Index

A

a posteriori arguments vii, viii, 22
a priori arguments vi–vii, viii, 22
aesthetic argument, Augustine's
    71–2, 74, 78–9
aetiological myths 33–4
afterlife 39
    body/soul relationship and 40–6
    Hick's theodicy and 85
    personal identity and 47–60
algorithms 51
analogies 30
    analogical view of religious
        language 30–1
    Ramsey's theory of 31
analytic propositions viii, 9, 22
Anselm of Canterbury, St 2
    on faith and reason 15–16
    ontological argument 1–4, 17
anthropomorphism 21
anti-realism 17
Aquinas, St Thomas
    analogical view of religious
        language 30–1
    beliefs about the soul 46
    development of Augustine's
        theodicy 72
    on God's existence and evil 65
    on ontological argument 7–8
archetypes 32
arguments, logical **vi–vii**
Aristotle 45
    and the soul 45
atheists 2, 16
atman 53
Atwater, P. M. H.
    on near-death experiences 58
Augustine of Hippo, St 68
Augustinian theodicies 68
    Augustine's argument 69–72
    developments of Augustine's
        argument 72–4
    strengths of 75
    weaknesses of 76–9
Ayer, A. J.
    and verification principle 23–4

B

Barth, Karl
    on ontological argument 17
Blackmore, Susan
    'dying brain' hypothesis 59–60
bliks 27–8, 28
body/soul relationship 39

dualism and 41, 44–6
materialism and 40–1, 41–4
Braithwaite, R. B.
    on religious language 36
Buddhism and rebirth 54
Bultman, Rudolph
    on religious language 34

C

Calvin, John
    development of Augustine's
        theodicy 72–4, 76
Cartesian dualism 45–6
Christianity
    resurrection in 48
    and the soul 50
    view of the person 46
cognitive neuroscience 59
cognitive religious language 21
coherent notion of the soul 60, 61
consciousness 40
    and personal identity 50–1
    reincarnation and rebirth and
        54, 55
    scientific theories of 43, 44, 51–2
contingent 14
counterfactual hypothesis 84
creation
    Augustine on 69, 71, 77
    creation myths 33–4
    Gnosticism and 89
    God's role in 90–1
cross, as a symbol 32–3

D

Davies, Brian
    on evil as a substance 75
    on use of 'is' 12
Dawkins, Richard 42
    on biological materialism 42–4
    on ontological argument 18
death 39
    body/soul and existence after
        39–46
    and the free-will defence 81
    personal identity after 47–60
deductive arguments **vi–vii, vii, viii**
Descartes, René 5
    dualism of mind/body 45–6, 49
    ontological argument 5–7
determinism and free will 78, 82
determinists 82
DNA 43
dualism 40, 41, 44–6, 49, 50
'dying brain' hypothesis 59–60

E

empiricism 23, 24
epistemic distance 84
equivocal language 23
eschatological verification 28
evidential problem of evil 66–7
evil
    Augustinian theodicies 68–79
    concept of 63
    free-will defence 79–82, 88–9
    Hick's theodicy 83–8
    natural and moral evil and faith
        94–5
    problem of 64–7
    process philosophy and 90–4
    theodicies on 67–8
evolution 43, 94
existence *see* God, existence of;
    personal existence

F

faith 15
    natural and moral evil and 94–5
    significance of ontological
        argument for 15–19
    and verification 28–9, 30
falsification principle 25–6
Flew, Antony
    falsification principle 25–6
    on Hare's idea of 'bliks' 28
    on Mitchell's ideas on beliefs 29
Forms, The (Plato) 44
free will
    Calvin on 73, 74
    determinism and 78
    justifying existence of evil 75, 88–9
    and origin of evil 70
free-will defence 74, 76, 79–82, 89
Frege, Gottlob
    first- and second-order
        predicates 11

G

Gasking, Douglas
    on existence of God 18
Gaunilo of Marmoutiers
    criticism of Anselm's ontological
        argument 4–5
ghosts 56
Gilkey, Langdon on use of myth 34
Gnosticism 68, 82, 89
God, existence
    of evil and 64–5
    ontological argument for 1–19

God of classical theism 1, 5, 64
Greyson Scale of near-death experiences 57
Griffin, David process theodicy 90–3

H

Hameroff, Stuart
on consciousness 51
hard materialism 40
Hare, R. M.
on religious language 27–8
Hartshorne, Charles
on ontological argument 15
Hick, John 15
on Augustinian theodicy 76–7, 77
on necessary existence 15
replica theory 47–9
'vale of soul-making' theodicy 83–8, 89
on verification principle 28
Hinduism and reincarnation 53–4
Hume, David 8
on God and evil 64
on ontological argument 8–9
hypoxia 59

I

immortality 39
inconsistent triad 65
inductive arguments vii, viii
infinite possibilities 13
intentions, extensions of 10, 11
Irenaean theodicy 74, 83, 86
Irenaeus
on Gnosticism 82
'is', meaning of 12

J

Jaff, Aniela
on symbols 32–3
James, William
on determinism and free will 78
jiva 53–4
Jung, Carl Gustav
on symbols 32

K

Kant, Immanuel 9
on determinism and free will 78
on ontological argument 9–10, 16
and propositions viii
karma 53, 54
Kierkegaard, Søren
on free-will defence 79

L

language games 35–6
Leibnitz, Gottfried W.
theodicy of 74

Locke, John
on personal identity 50–1
logical arguments vi–vii
logical positivists 22
verification principle 22–4, 26–9
logical problem of evil 64–5
logically necessary statements vi

M

Mackie, J. L.
on free will 80, 82, 89
logical problem of evil 64
Malcolm, Norman
on ontological argument 12–13
Manichaeism 68
materialism 40
and body/soul relationship 40–1, 41–4
replica theory 47–9
maximal excellence concept 14
meaningfulness 21
mediums 56–7
memes 44
memories of past lives 55
metaphors 31, 33
Midgely, Mary
on wickedness and evil 88
mind 41, 45, 50
see also soul
Mitchell, Basil
on religious beliefs 28–9, 30
moksha 53
Momen, Moojan
on faith 19
Moody, Dr Raymond
research into near-death experiences 57
moral evil 63, 71, 75, 83, 93, 94–5
Morse, Melvin
research on near-death-experiences 58
myths 33
religious language as myth 33–4

N

natural evil 63, 71, 75, 83, 93, 94–5
near-death experiences (NDEs) 57–60
necessary existence of God 3, 6, 12–13, 15
non-cognitive language 27
nous 45

O

ontological argument 1
Anselm's version 1–5
Descartes' version 5–7
Gaunilo's criticism of Anselm's 4–5

key objections to 7–12
responses to objections 12–15
significance for faith 15–19

P

Parable of the Freedom Fighter (Mitchell) 28–9
Parable of the Gardener (Wisdom) 26
paradoxes 9
Penrose, Roger
on consciousness 51
perfections 6
Persinger, Dr
on near-death experiences 59
personal existence 39
personal identity 39
and death 47–60
nature and existence of the soul 39–46
philosophy, nature of vi
Pinn, Anthony
on Hick's theodicy 87
Plantinga, Alvin
on free will 80
possible worlds notion 13–14
Plato 44
and the Forms 44
plenitude, principle of 71
possible worlds 13–14
post-mortem existence 52, 56
predestination
Augustine on 69
Calvin on 73, 74, 77
strengths of theme of 75
predicates 6
existence as a predicate 6, 8, 9–11
first- and second- order 11
premises vi
Price, H. H.
dream world afterlife 52
principle of plenitude 71
privatio boni 70–1
privation 69, 70, 72
probability vii
problem of evil 64
Augustinian theodicies 68–79
evidential 66–7
free-will defence 79–82, 88–9
Hick's theodicy 83–8
logical 64–5
process thought and 90–4
theodicies in response to 67–8
process philosophy 90–4
property 15
property dualism 40
propositions vi
analytic and synthetic viii, 9–10, 22
verification 22–30

Proslogion (Anselm) **1–3, 17**
psyche 45
psychosomatic view of the person 46

quantum theory 51

Ramsey, Ian
 theory of analogy **31**
Randall, J. R.
 on religious language **32**
reason vi
 faith and **15–17**
rebirth 52–3, 54, 55
recreation theory **47–9**
reductio ad absurdum **arguments
 vii, 3**
reincarnation 51, 52–4, 55
religious language **21**
 different views of **30–6**
 falsification principle **25–6**
 possibility of meaningful talk
  about God **37**
 verification principle **22–4, 29–30**
 verification principle challenged
  26–9
replica theory 47–9
resurrection 47
 in Christianity **48**
replica theory **47–8, 48–9**
Reynolds, Pam **59**
Rowe, William
 evidential problem of evil **66–7**
Russell, Bertrand **10**
 and ontological argument **10–11,
 16**
Ryle, Gilbert
 on the soul **41–2**

Savage, William
 on reincarnation **55**
Schleiermacher, F. D. E.
 on Augustinian theodicies **76**
self-consciousness **55**
sin
 Aquinas on **72**
 Augustine on **68, 70–1**
 Calvin on **73**
soft materialism **40**
soul 39
 after death **49–54**
 coherence of notion of **60–1**
 Hick's 'vale of soul-making'
  theodicy **83–8**
 is there evidence for existence
  of? **61**
 Manichaeism and **68**
 nature and existence of **39–46**
spiritualism 56–7
'stone tape' theory **56**
substances 44
 evil as a substance? **70, 75**
suffering **63**
 Augustine's explanation for **70–1**
 evidential problem of evil **66–7**
 Hick's theodicy and **87, 88**
 process philosophy on **91–2, 92, 93**
Swinburne, Richard
 on free will **79–80, 81**
 on soft materialism **40**
syllogisms 10
symbols 31
 religious language as symbolic
  31–3
synthetic propositions viii, 22
 existence as **9–10**

tautologies **vi**
theodicies 67–8
 in Augustinian tradition **68–79**
 free-will defence **79–82, 88–9**
 Hick's 'vale of soul-making' **83–8**
 process **90–4**
Tillich, Paul
 on religious language **31–2**

univocal language 23

Vardy, Peter
 on human development **86**
verification 22
verification principle 22–3
 challenges to **26–9**
 development by Ayer **23–4**
 falsification principle response
  25–6
 religious responses to **29–30**
via negativa **29**
Vienna Circle **22**

Wisdom, John
 Parable of the Gardener **26**
Wittgenstein, Ludwig
 language games **35–6**